PRACTICAL APPLICATIONS OF AGENT-BASED TECHNOLOGY

Edited by **Haiping Xu**

Practical Applications of Agent-Based Technology
Edited by Haiping Xu

Published by InTech
Janeza Trdine 9, 51000 Rijeka, Croatia

Publishing Process Manager Ivona Lovric

Technical Editor Teodora Smiljanic

Cover Designer InTech Design Team

Additional hard copies can be obtained from orders@intechopen.com

Practical Applications of Agent-Based Technology, Edited by Haiping Xu
p. cm.
ISBN 978-953-51-0276-2

For EU product safety concerns:
IN TECH d.o.o., Prolaz Marije Krucifikse Kozulić 3, 51000 Rijeka, Croatia,
info@intechopen.com or visit our website at intechopen.com.

Meet the editor

Dr Haiping Xu received the Ph.D. degree in Computer Science from the University of Illinois at Chicago, IL, in 2003. Prior to that, he successively worked with Shen-Yan Systems Technology, Inc. and Hewlett-Packard Co., as a Software Engineer, in Beijing, China. Since 2003, he has been with the University of Massachusetts Dartmouth, where he is currently an Associate Professor at the Computer and Information Science Department, and a Director of the Concurrent Software Engineering Laboratory (CSEL). His research has been supported by the U.S. National Science Foundation (NSF) and the U.S. Marine Corps. His major research interests include distributed software engineering, formal methods, multi-agent systems, electronic commerce, data mining, service-oriented systems, cybersecurity, and cloud computing.

Contents

Preface

Over the past decade, there has been a strong revival of interest in agent-based technology, with a recognition that it impacts many areas such as artificial intelligence, distributed computing, and software engineering. Agent-based technology can be used to solve a variety of business and technology problems. Examples of such applications include electronic commerce, grid computing, social networks, and adaptive virtual environment. In an agent-based system, software agents with sufficient intelligence and autonomy are adopted to perform tasks such as sensing, planning, scheduling, reasoning and decision-making. An agent can either work independently or coordinate with other agents to accomplish tasks and missions. In the former case, an agent typically generates a set of goals based on its motivation, and also a list of plans for achieving its goals. In the later case, a collection of agents are structured as a multi-agent system (MAS), where a coordination model based on message passing among agents is defined to provide a uniform interface for their interactions. In this book, we provide a collection of practical applications of agent-based technology. Chapter 1 demonstrates how agent-based technology can be applied to smart distribution grid operation. It presents an agent-based architecture which can be developed to support the smooth modernization of the power distribution grids. Chapter 2 discusses how to resolve conflicts in resource federation with agent negotiation. A scenario of resource federation in grid computing is illustrated to show the adoption of creative negotiation for conflict resolution. Chapter 3 and 4 provide two application examples of agent-based technology in electronic commerce, where homogeneous and heterogeneous agents are defined and adopted for electronic auctions (Chapter 3), and a multi-issue e-negotiation system is developed for electronic commerce (Chapter 4). Chapter 5 presents an innovative application of intelligent agents in adaptive virtual environments. By using intelligent agents, a three-dimensional (3D) virtual environment can be tuned into an adaptive system, which improves the quality of human-computer interface. Chapter 6 provides another example of using intelligent agent to find the shortest path between two points in a changing drawing environment.

Although we present quite a few practical application examples of using agent-based technology in this book, the collection of such application areas is far from completion. The purpose of this book is to provide examples of recent advances in agent-based systems and demonstrate how agent-based technology can be used to solve practical problems. It is our hope that this book will not only help the researchers and practitioners to understand the practical usage of agent-based technology, but also provides them hints of using agent-based technology in innovative ways.

This book has been a collaborative effort, which wouldn't be possible for us to complete it without the substantial contribution and generous assistance we received from many people. We are most grateful, of course, to the authors of the chapters for the quality of their research. We are also especially grateful for the generous support from the InTech Open Access Publisher. At InTech, we thank all those who assisted in this book, especially Ivona Lovric for her much hard work on communicating with the authors and helping put all chapters together.

Haiping Xu, PhD
Associate Professor
Director of Concurrent Software Engineering Laboratory
Computer and Information Science Department
University of Massachusetts Dartmouth Massachusetts
USA

1

Agent-Based System Applied to Smart Distribution Grid Operation

D. Issicaba, M. A. Rosa, W. Franchin and J. A. Peças Lopes
Institute for Systems and Computer Engineering of Porto (INESC Porto)
Faculty of Engineering, University of Porto
Portugal

1. Introduction

The twenty-first century has been called software century by some software engineering researchers. The challenge for humanity is to improve the quality of life without making unsustainable demands on the environment. Agent-oriented software engineering is an important emerging technology that can cope with the ever-increasing software complexity of the technical world (Liu & Antsaklis, 2009).

This chapter presents an agent-based architecture which was developed to support the smooth modernization of the power distribution grids. This architecture copes with the smart grid paradigm (ETP, 2008) and leads to changes in the grid operation rules, control and protection, as well as grid infrastructure. The main target of the architecture is to distribute decisions related to smart grid operation and to improve service adequacy and security. Hence, a complex environment simulation is designed to emulate the distribution grid operation and evaluate the impact of agent's plans of action. The environment itself is modeled using a combined discrete-continuous simulation approach (Law, 2007) in which steady-state and dynamic aspects of the electrical behavior of distribution grids are represented in a detail way.

The simulation platform was designed according to the software engineering methodology Prometheus (Pagdgham & Winikoff, 2007). The resultant architecture follows a block-oriented paradigm in which the power distribution grid is divided into blocks for protection and control purposes. Such paradigm shows to be considerably convenient to support the transition from actual grids to smart grids. In addition, it allows software agents to be assigned to the management and control of blocks of the grid, given life to "block agents". Agents are also assigned to entities which are capable of affecting the distribution grid operation, such as distributed generators (DGs), special loads, and electric vehicles (EVs). All agents are modeled according to the Belief-Desire-Intention (BDI) paradigm (Bratman et al., 1988) and implemented using JASON (Bordini et al., 2007), the open source interpreter of an extended version of AgentSpeak. A didactic case study illustrates how service adequacy and security can be improved with the application of the proposed agent-based decision planning.

1.1 Problem statement

Electrical power grids are designed to provide electricity with a certain level of adequacy and security. Like most of the systems developed by the human beings, the electrical power grids evolve based on trends motivated by economical, environmental and societal drivers. Recently, such drivers have caused the advent of well-established initiatives especially concerned with these systems as the Modern Grid Initiative (NETL, 2007), the IntelliGrid Initiative (EPRI, 2005), and the European Smart Grids Technology Platform (ETP, 2008). In general terms, these initiatives try to foster on different extends the deployment of decentralized control and management solutions, the integration of renewable and distributed energy resources, as well as the modernization of the power grids. The deployment of decentralized control and management solutions has increased in the past few years. The integration of renewable and distributed energy resources has also increased, particulary in what concerns wind power in Europe. The modernization of the power grids is a gradual process which can be observed in countries with more economical power.

The technical challenges created by this context embrace several power engineering related fields of expertise as power electronics, communication, information technology, and software engineering. Additionally, the quoted drivers have been influencing power engineering itself in terms of its areas (long-term planning, mid-term planning, short-term or operational planning, operation, control and protection), as well as its structure/organization (generation, transmission, and distribution). In particular, the distribution grid operation and control might stand as one of the most promising to change areas. As a matter of fact, most of the interruptions in supply are caused by problems at the distribution grids which lacks monitoring and control devices in comparison with the transmission grids. Furthermore, distribution grids are the main locus for distributed energy resources (DERs) such as DGs, energy storage devices and controllable loads. At last, the proposed modernization along with the integration of DERs must guarantee service adequacy and security. Such target involves re-evaluating distribution grid operation and control under the presence of DERs.

Nowadays, the capability of DERs are yet not exploited at their most. In fact, traditionally distribution utilities employ the practice of tripping DGs after the occurrence of a fault. Hence, islanded operation is avoided both for sustaining the operation after a fault or for restorative purposes. Therefore, in order to profit from the benefits DERs can provide to the grid operation and to foster the large-scale integration of DERs, control strategies for the emergency operation of distribution grids with DERs must be developed. Furthermore, the impact of these control strategies in the distribution grid performance must be evaluated to foster the integration of such strategies into the operation procedures. Finally, these control strategies must be designed in order to make it possible their gradual implementation, without requiring great changes in the simple and cheap structure actual distributions grids are operated.

1.2 Motivation

Agent-based technology provides the most suitable paradigm to allow a smooth transition from the actual distribution grids to smart distribution grids. Such statement is justified by the followings.

1. The increase in complexity and size of the distribution grids bring up the need for *distributed intelligence* and *local solutions*, which fall into the scope of agent-based technology.
2. Smart/modern grid design concepts related with operation and communication can be tested through an agent-based modeling and simulation.
3. Decentralization, autonomy and active management are properties inherent of a system developed under the agent-oriented philosophies. Furthermore, an adequate agent-based modeling can produce flexible, extensible, and robust systems[1] (McArthur et al., 2007). All these features are of most importance to a smooth modernization of distribution grids.

The tangible product of the work is an agent-based simulation platform where the smart grid operation and control solutions can be tested and evaluated. The target group of the work includes software engineering researchers and power engineers.

2. Brief discussion about the state of the art

Regarding applications related to this research, some works must be emphasized. In (Rehtanz, 2003), the application of autonomous systems concepts and intelligent agents theory for power systems operation and control is discussed. In (Amin, 2001), a conceptual framework for a power system self-healing infrastructure is envisaged. In (Nagata & Sasaki, 2002; Nagata et al., 2004; 2003a;b), the authors presented a multi-agent system designed for distribution systems restoration. This works abstracts network buses as agents, along with a so called facilitation agent who is responsible for aiding negotiation processes among bus agents. A more decentralized approach for distribution system restoration is shown in (Solanki et al., 2007), where switches, loads and upstream links are abstracted as agents. In (Hossack et al., 2003), the agent abstraction was utilized to integrate tools for post-fault diagnoses. In (Baxevanos & Labridis, 2007), a control and protection framework using agent-based technology is proposed. An autonomous regional active network management system is introduced and discussed in (Davidson & McArthur, 2007). This work provides an interesting discussion about requirements for practical active management of distribution grids. In (Dimeas & Hatziargyriou, 2005), entities related with the control of micro grids are abstracted as agents and their interactions modeled. Although in this work the agent-based modeling was utilized, the resultant control architecture maintain the hierarchical structure applied in the micro grid (and multi-micro grid) concept. A distributed electric power system simulator environment is presented in (Hopkinson et al., 2006). Finally, an intelligent agent-based environment to coordinate maintenance schedule discussions is introduced in (Rosa et al., 2009), and a modern computing environment for power system reliability assessment is presented in (Rosa et al., 2010).

In general, these works do not describe the deployment of a software engineering methodology. In addition, none of them provide one of the most important issue for the practical implementation and acceptance of agent-based technology in distribution grid applications: an environment which emulates the system operation to evaluate the agent-based solutions according to standardized (and regulated) distribution grid performance indices (see (Issicaba et al., 2011) for details). This work introduces such

[1] Conceptually, flexibility is the ability to respond correctly to different (dynamic) situations. Extensibility connotes the ability of augmenting, upgrading or adding new functionality to a system. Finally, robustness stands for a degree of system fault tolerance.

a platform as well as discusses the physical/hardware implementation of the proposed solutions, how the environment is influenced by them in terms of modeling, and some agent interactions necessary to solve problems related to smart distribution grid operation.

3. Distribution grid automation

Grid, in the electrical engineering vocabulary, means the infrastructure used to deliver electric energy over an area. As a consequence, it connects the whole chain of the electricity business from the high voltage generation and transmission facilities up to houses and industries. Hence, large amounts of electric energy are produced in the generation facilities and transported through the transmission grid. By means of the distribution grid, these amounts of electric energy are partitioned and distributed to the customers over large coverage areas, usually under the concession of an electric distribution utility.

Distribution grid automation consists of a set of technologies that enable an electric distribution utility to remotely monitor, coordinate an operate distribution grid components, such as circuit breakers, reclosers, autosectionalizers, and so on, in a real-time mode from remote locations (Northcote-Green & Wilson, 2006). The main reason for the distribution grid automation may be sustained by the difficulties the utilities have in monitoring, coordinating and operating feeders everyday, manually. Usually, the remote controls are activated at a control room inside the electric distribution utility. It is interesting to notice the centralized concept behind this control principle which, in fact, is one of the automation measures adopted for reducing the utility man hour and man power.

One of the primary difficulties about managing a distribution grid starts with its extend. Usually, for each 1 km of transmission grid there are about 70 km of distribution grids, only considering an ordinary distribution utility around the world. Therefore, huge investments in distribution management system (DMS) including cooperation with other application systems such as network geographic information system, costumer information system and usually a large communication infrastructure are needed.

3.1 General aspects about the distribution grid automation

Before introducing any set of architectural solutions for the control and automation of distribution grids under the smart grid paradigm, it is important to highlight some others existing initiatives such as the GridWise Architecture Council (`http://www.gridwiseac.org/`), EPRI IntelliGrid (`http://intelligrid.epri.com/`) and Utility AMI (`http://www.utilityami.org/`). These initiatives along with the U.S. National Institute of Standards and Technology (`http://www.nist.gov/`) and other stakeholders have constructed a reference model for smart grid interoperability of energy technology and information technology operation with electric power system, end-use applications and load (IEEEP2030, 2011). Besides the goals and general directives, such model identify the logical information that can be interchanged between entities, communication interfaces, and data flow. Such information is of major interest to evaluate the complexity in operating power systems. As an instance, Fig. 1 shows the distribution grid domain, its entities and related communication interfaces of this model. Apart from these initiatives, some European projects can also be quoted such as the InovGrid Project, which proposes an hierarchical technical architecture focused on micro grids and multi-micro grid concepts (Cunha et al., 2008).

Henceforth, it is recommended that control and automation solutions should be compatible and/or as complementary as possible to the existing specifications, and also foster their decentralization and extensibility. In terms of distribution grid network management, as already mentioned, the current DMS platforms have evolved in order to integrate and/or cooperate with other systems, mainly focusing on the whole set of activities around the distribution grid operation. The evolution of the DMS into the electric distribution utilities is discussed. Fig. 2 highlights the typical pathways from which DMS have evolved around the world.

From the control and automation perspective, the distribution grid has been evolved from the substation automation to feeder automation. Fig. 3 shows the main distribution grid equipments involved in this evolution.

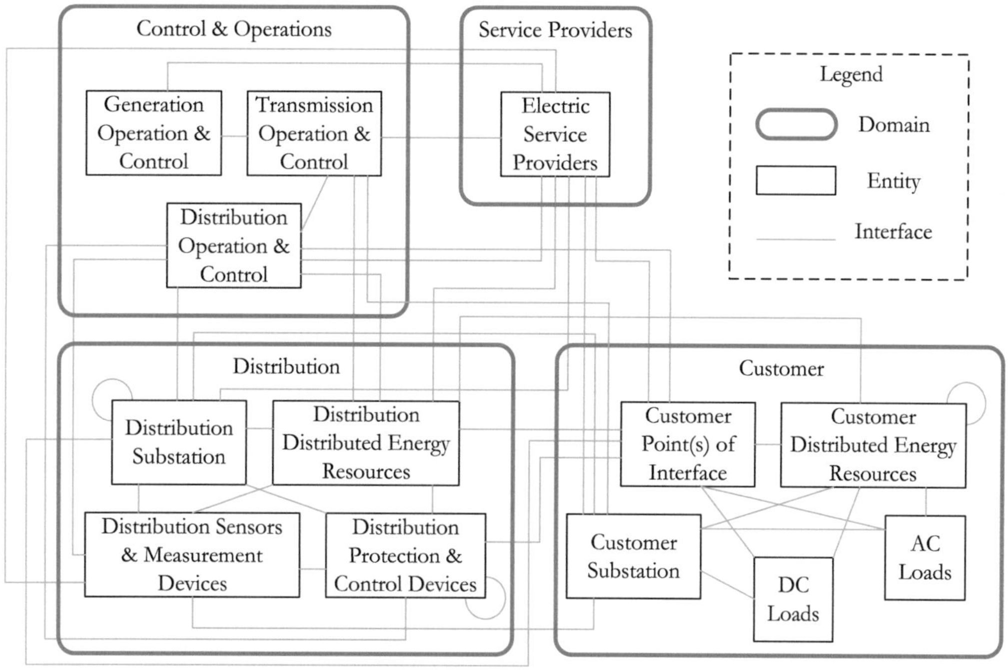

Fig. 1. Distribution grid interoperability perspective. Adapted from (IEEEP2030, 2011).

The target is to improve the grid performance, mitigate the impact of interruptions, diminish interruption times, reduce crew personnel and its operational costs, and so forth. Furthermore, the ongoing integration of DERs in the distribution grids have introduced challenges to distribution grid control and protection.

3.2 Towards a decentralized distribution grid automation

The distribution grid is subjected to random conditions linked to the environment such as weather behavior, presence of vegetation near the overhead network, interaction with human-being and so forth. From a centralized DMS perspective, the decision-making process involves directly at least one operator (human intervention) which should decide whether to change or not the operational status of a remote controlled device. Additionally, it requires

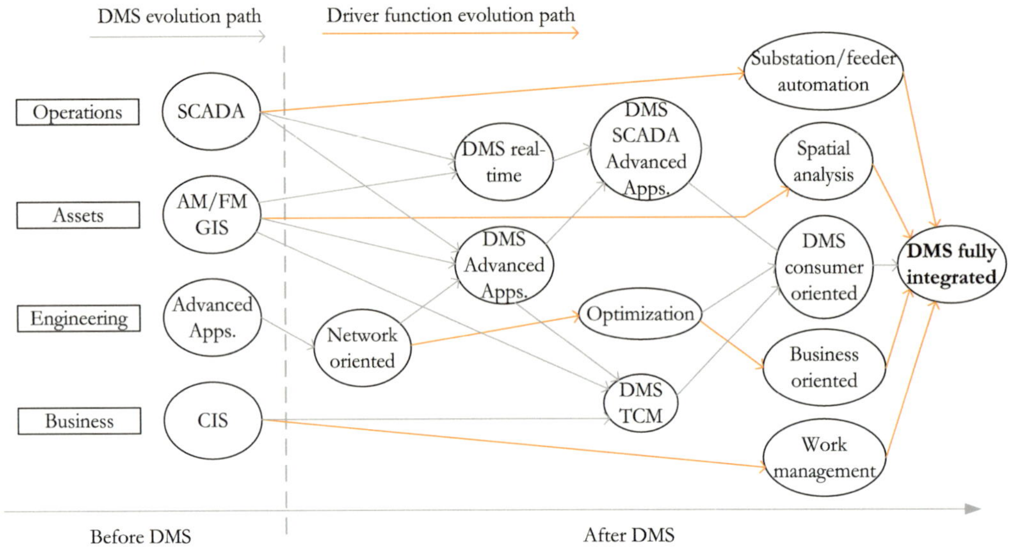

Fig. 2. Typical pathways of DMS evolution (Northcote-Green & Wilson, 2006).

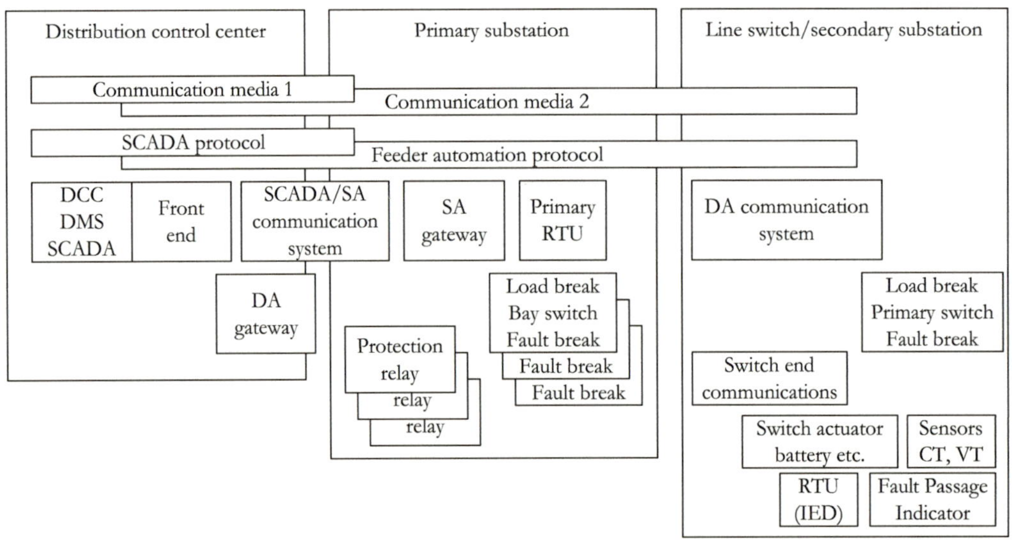

Fig. 3. Components of distribution grid control and automation (Northcote-Green & Wilson, 2006).

precise information that cover almost every possible equipment condition and surrounding environment variables necessary to preserve, not only the asset integrity, but also the safety of the utility staff. In general, a considerable number of field electricians trained to interact with the network components is needed.

Conversely to the centralized solution commonly applied in several utilities, the proposed solutions are based on a decentralized perspective, where the remote control actions are

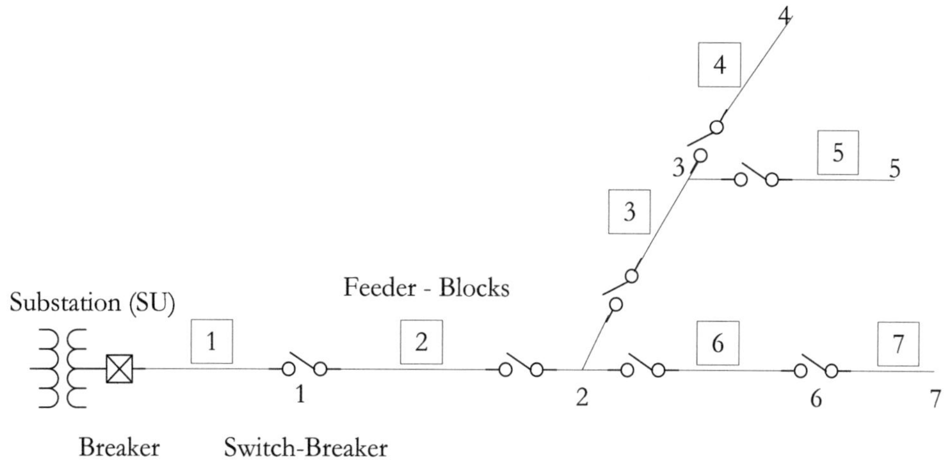

Fig. 4. Distribution feeder divided into blocks.

supported by an agent-based architecture. In fact, the automation decision tree introduced in (Northcote-Green & Wilson, 2006) revels that the current distribution grid automation infrastructure that allows a centralized control is entirely prepared for decentralized approaches. Therefore, the ordinary steps to the implementation of automation for any manual switch can be revisited in order to clarify the requirements for decentralized solutions under an agent-based paradigm.

Let us discuss some properties about the distribution feeders. From the construction point of view, it is mandatory to understand the design of a a distribution feeder, and afterwards it is possible to think about feeder automation. Fig. 4 presents a small representation of a distribution feeder and its natural structure divided by switches. As it can be seen, the distribution feeder starts from the substation breaker and it goes towards each switch, passing through intersections such as point 2, from where the feeder is split in others sub-feeders or laterals. One of the basic functions of each switch is to sectionalize the feeder in several parts firstly for construction purposes, and then afterwards for control purposes. At this point, it is possible to say that the feeder is composed by several individual blocks separated by different types of switches.

Historically, switches between blocks were operated manually. However, in a first automation step, mechanical actuators were included to allow local or remote control actions over a switch. Another particular point about switches is that they must be equipped to act under load conditions, which in fact is a restriction of the switches installed in most of the grids. Essentially, the first step enables the second step, where it is necessary to control the switch by an electronic control unit, or to control the switch by manual pushbuttons. Through this pathway of an electronic control unit installed upon the switch actuator it is possible to implement a remote control interfaced by a communication system. Thus, the option for switch-breaker automation can be based on a local intelligence allowing them to act automatically under the decision of an agent and under the supervision of an operator. Obviously, decision making processes can be implemented, either under an intelligent agent paradigm using devices in a server/computer of each block, or under a combination with both local block agent and central decision making with human intervention remotely.

Now, in order to illustrate the automation process, consider an automated system for switching all switch-breakers of the Fig. 4, where the main goal is to minimize the number of interruptions in each block. In this case, it is necessary to establish a goal model for the system and identify a set of rules in order to achieve the goals. Assuming that each block is an agent, it is also necessary to establish a cooperation process and a way of communication between them. So far, it was not mentioned about which is the environment of our block agents, and how they can percept and act changing the environment. This demands a formalization based on software architecture engineering, which is a key factor that will affect the whole implementation. Next section will explore in detail the Prometheus methodology to define the architecture of the automation proposal.

4. Proposed multi-agent architecture

The first step in building any complex system is to formalize the reasons for which this system must be built. However, specifying *goals* over the distribution grid operation can be a slippery task. In fact, despite of achieving acceptable *states of affair*, the goals must agree with the mission of the utility as an enterprize, respect grid standards and regulations, foster sustainability, and protect the interests of customers and stakeholders. Furthermore, goals can vary considerably depending upon the utility policies.

By following the Prometheus methodology (Pagdgham & Winikoff, 2007), a goal map for the proposed design was specified. We emphasize that the resultant set of goals is not complete in the sense of approaching all issues of distribution grid operation. Conversely, the goals were developed as general as possible with focus on tacking critical matters of the distribution grid operation and the smart grid paradigm.

Fig. 5 depicts the main goals applied in developing the proposed design. Similarly to any cognitive mapping, the top-down analysis shows causality from abstract to tangible concepts. Hence, the goal map includes technical matters such as to `protect the integrity of the equipments` and to `operate under high levels of service adequacy and security`, as well as smart grid matters such as to `foster DERs to participate in the operation issues`. As expected, some sub-goals already suggest that an agent abstraction should be assigned to the blocks of the distribution grid. For instance, when a sustained fault occurs in a distribution feeder, fault isolation is achieved by separating the faulted block from the remaining network. Then, service restoration is endeavored to connect as much blocks as possible to alternative supplies, aiming at minimizing the number of customers under service interruption. The sub-goal `DG islanded operation` itself points even more to a block-oriented paradigm. In order to minimize customer interruptions and foster the exploitation of DER capabilities, DG islanded operation procedures have been verified. Given the spatial distributed signature of DGs and their restricted capacity in supplying feeder's customers, DG islanded operation is expected to be achieved only in certain set of blocks of the grid.

After going ahead with the Prometheus phases, the functionalities and agents illustrated in Fig. 6 and 7 were derived. The functionality names are self-explainable as well as they are related with the goals and possible percepts/actions according to the diagrams. Agents are assigned to the distribution system operator (DSO), DGs, EVs, and loads. These agents are then modeled as clients of a management and control service provided by `block agents`. The percepts `node voltage`, `switch status`, `neigh-power flow`, and `FPI` stand for

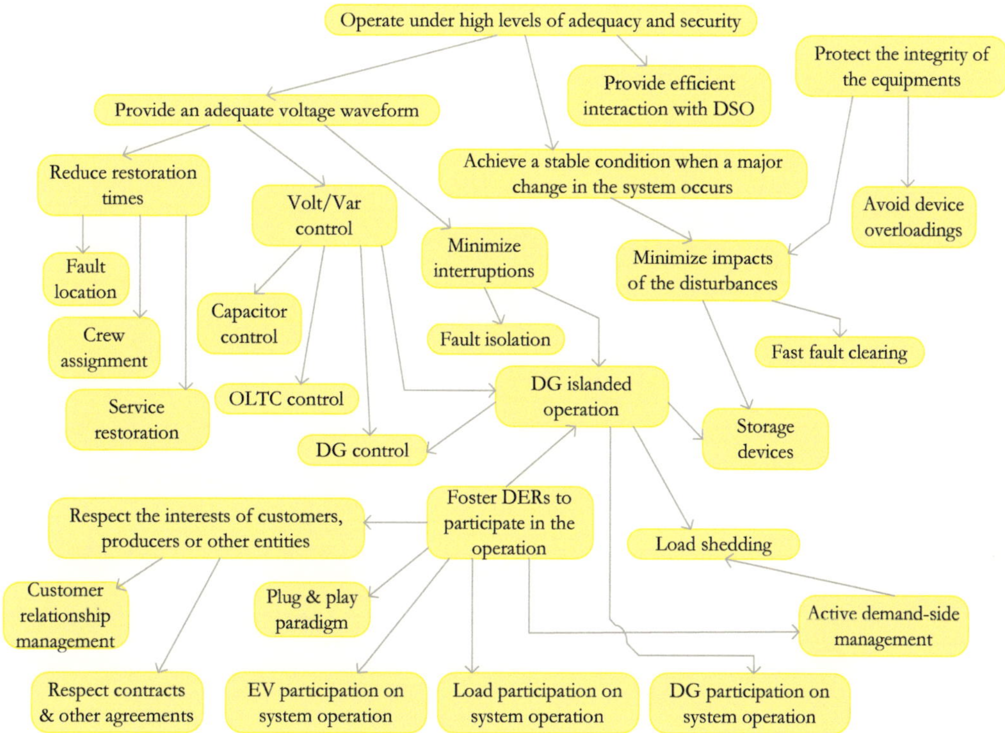

Fig. 5. Goal overview for the agent-based architecture.

electric voltages, operational status of a switch (open, close, in-service, out-of-service), power flow at an aggregated component, and fault passage indicator, respectively. On the other hand, `client subscription` and `client update` denote percepts referred to client attempts in subscribing or updating subscriptions to the block management and control services.

In order to pursue all goals, each `block agent` is responsible for feeding and sharing information with its neighboring agents through the electric utility communication system. Hence, actions related to searching for clients and neighbors as well as the information flow rules are designed as presented in (Issicaba et al., 2010). Other actions, such as `send Q setpoint` and `send tap setpoint` are applied when inadequate node voltages are perceived. For instance, if local low node voltages are identified, the tap of a capacitor component can be increased step by step up to a limit aiming at voltage correction. DG control setpoint conveyance through `send P setpoint` actions are also performed to reduce the power flow at the DG ties in case the entity representing the DG agrees contractually with such scheme. This reduction is crucial in case DG islanded operation is desired. At last, DMS report sending actions are triggered when protection plans are changed or outages are assigned.

Since JASON (Bordini et al., 2007) was utilized to interpreted AgentSpeak coded agents, percepts are represented by literals, saved in a belief base, and used to trigger plans selected

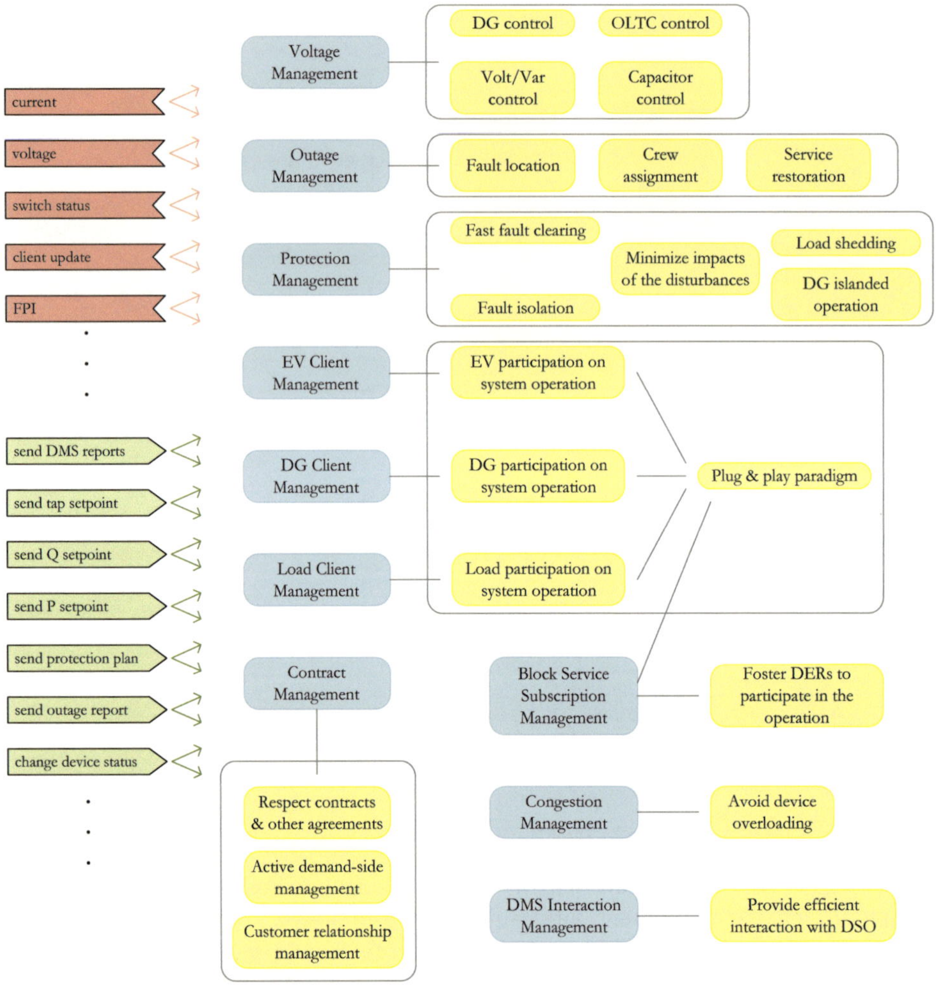

Fig. 6. Role overview for the agent-based architecture.

from a large library. As an example of planning, let us take the sub-goal `DG islanded operation`. In case a sustained fault current is identified, breaker action from standard automation must clear and isolate the fault leaving some blocks disconnected from the main grid. Therefore, to cooperate in order to maximize the customers served by DG islanded operation, each `block agent` cyclically evaluates the ability of its assignee to survive the islanding process when connected to the downstream remaining grids. If there is not enough client power reserve to supply the remaining grid, the `block agent` will set a plan linking the breaker action to its own isolation actions. This increases the chances of the remaining `block agents` to achieve DG islanded operation and minimizes customer interruptions. This particular plan was implemented similar to the followings.

```
@DGislanded_operation_plan04
+!protection_planning_instance
:  reserve(PathId,MWreserve,MWLoading,MVARreserve,MVARLoading)
```

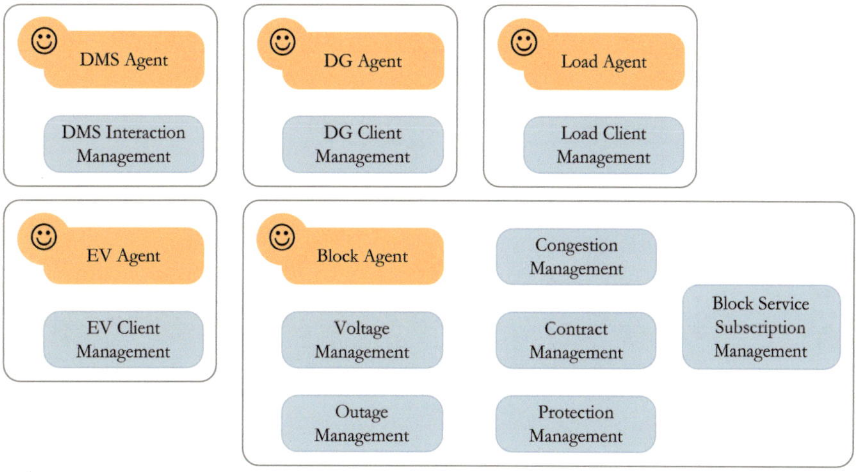

Fig. 7. Agent role overview.

```
[visited=no] & (MWreserve < MWLoading | MVARreserve < MVARLoading)
<- setplan(fault,PathId,isolate_itself).
```

All goals and sub-goals must have at least a plan to tackle them. These plans are activated repeatedly depending upon their own contexts and the agent's interaction with the environment.

5. Environment modeling: emulating the distribution grid operation

One of the key aspects about agents is that they are situated in an environment. In the proposed architecture, agents perceive and act upon the basic protection and control layer of the distribution grid. Therefore, the distribution grid itself is the environment and the architecture must utilize the sensors and actuators available in the distribution grid automation. Of course, since our architecture is aimed to a real-world application, a rigorous model to simulating the environment is required before any field test. This leads to a complex software environment modeling featured as partially observable, stochastic, sequential/time-dependent, dynamic and discrete-event/continuous-time (Law, 2007; Russell & Norvig, 2002).

Hence, an object-oriented modeling was developed for each entity of the distribution grid automation. This modeling was based upon works in the area (Manzoni, 2005) and elements from power system analysis software (GDFSUEZ & RTE, 2004). Over the grid representation, a combined discrete-continuous simulation model (Law, 2007) was devised where the distribution grid operation is abstracted as a sequence of operation states marked by state transitions. Discrete state transitions are caused by events such as the failure of a component or DG unit, fault-clearing breaker action, and relay-based load shedding. Also, electrical continuously changing state variables are modeled by differential equations and solved through numerical integration. The operation states are sequentially evaluated up to the convergence of performance indices following a Sequential Monte Carlo approach (Rubinstein & Kroese, 2008). Numerical integration was implemented using the fourth-order

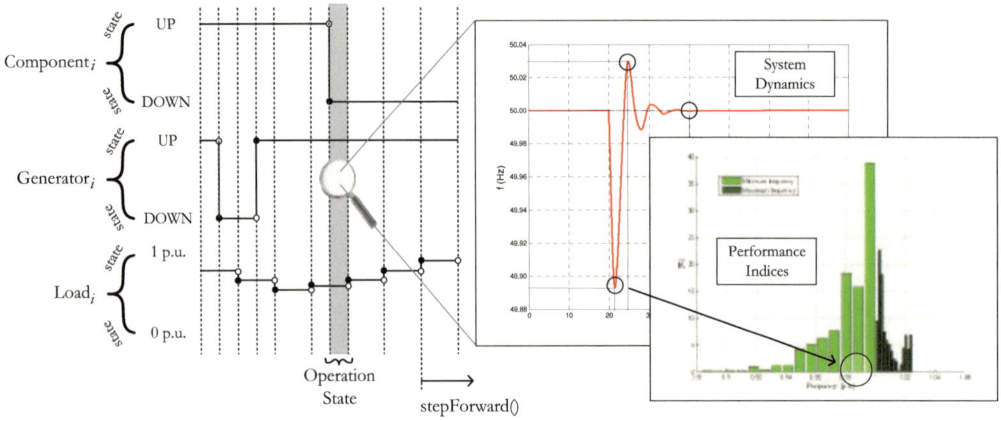

Fig. 8. Sequence of operation states in the combined discrete-continuous simulation model.

Runge-Kutta method from the Flanagan's Java Scientific Library (Flanagan, 2011). Fig. 8 illustrates how the operation states are created and evaluated in the simulation model.

More descriptive, the stochastic failure/repair cycle of grid components and DG units is represented by two-state Markov models, as introduced in (Billinton & Jonnavithula, 1996). DG units and network components state residence times are assumed to be exponentially distributed, and are sampled using the equation below (Billinton & Li, 1994)

$$T \leftarrow -\frac{1}{\lambda} \ln U \tag{1}$$

where T is the state residence time of the component/unit, λ is the transition rate out from the current state, and U is a uniformly distributed random number which is sampled at $[0, 1]$. The loads patterns are represented using a deterministic load model consisting on 8736 peak load percentage levels (Subcommittee, 1979), each associated to one hour of the year. From an electric steady-state perspective, components and DG units are modeled by their equivalent $\pi-$ and $PQ-$ representations (Kundur, 1993). The continuous-time dynamic behavior of the electrical and electromechanical variables follows the formulation presented in (Machowski et al., 2008).

During simulation, when a state transition is assigned, protection and control actions may take place in an attempt to improve the system operation. These actions include the basic distribution automation actions plus those which were planned by the software agents. The agent's plans and actions are considered in the simulation model through interaction between the agent architecture and the environment, and following the structure depicted in Fig 9.

As suggested in (Bordini et al., 2007), the overall simulation platform is implemented such that AgentSpeak agents interact through speech-act based communication as well as with a shared environment coded in JAVA language. In this approach, the modeled environment named `DistributionGridEnv` extends JASON's environment class and works with a model class named `DistributionGridSimModel`, which in turn abstracts the combined discrete-continuous simulation. The classes `OperationState`, `StateComposer` and `StateEvaluator` are then responsible to abstract, produce, and evaluate operation states, while the `IndexComposer` class must update and manage the performance indices.

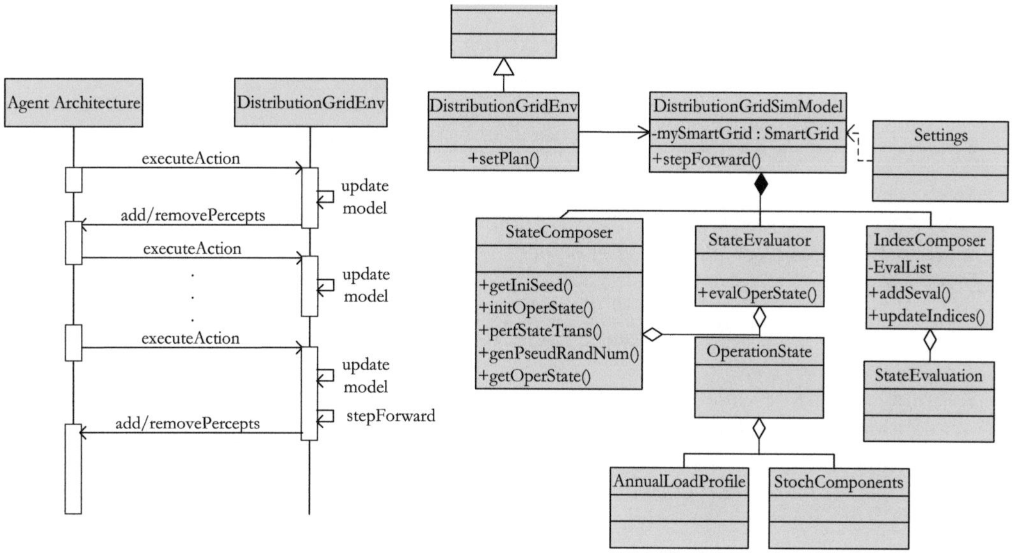

Fig. 9. Diagrams for the environment modeling and its interaction with the agent architecture.

In the whole simulation, each AgentSpeak agent follows a JASON's reasoning cycle where the environment's `executeAction` method is invoked to control elements of the distribution grid and/or to infer over protection planning. This may cause the model to be updated and *percepts* to be added or removed via `addPercept` or `removePercept` method invocation. In case a new *percept* is identified, its correspondent literal ℓ is added to the agent's belief base, as well as the triggering event $+\ell$ is added to the agent's event queue. Depending upon the contexts of the agent's plan library, the triggering event $+\ell$ may (or may not) cause *intentions* to be pursued and, eventually, more interactions with environment. Once all *intended means* are finished, the environment is allowed to step forward up to the next state transition instant by environment's `stepForward` method invocation. Note that this assumes that agent planning in the field is completed prior to the next state transition. This is considered a reasonable assumption given the step size and hourly resolution of load variation.

As previously remarked, the resultant sequence of operation states is evaluated in terms of performance indices. These performance indices involve both standardized distribution grid reliability indices as well as other user-tailored indices required to verify the impact of DERs on the grid operation. Usually, distribution grids are assessed from a customer service perspective rather than operation state classifications. Hence, customer service information is aggregated in systemic indices. The following systemic indices (Billinton & Wang, 1999; Brown, 2002) are applied in the performance evaluation of the electric distribution grids.

1. System Average Interruption Frequency Index: This index measures how many sustained interruptions an average customer will experience over the course of a year.

$$\text{SAIFI} = \frac{\text{Total number of customer interruptions}}{\text{Total number of customer served}} \quad (2)$$

2. System Average Interruption Duration Index: This index measures how many interruptions hours an average customer will experience over the course of a year.

$$\text{SAIDI} = \frac{\text{Sum of customer interruptions durations}}{\text{Total number of customer served}} \tag{3}$$

3. Customer Average Interruption Duration Index: This index measures how long an average interruption lasts over the course of a year.

$$\text{CAIDI} = \frac{\text{Sum of customer interruptions durations}}{\text{Total number of customer interruptions}} \tag{4}$$

4. Average Service Availability Index: This index measures the customer weighted availability of the system over the course of a year.

$$\text{ASAI} = \frac{\text{Customer hours of available service}}{\text{Customer hours demanded}} \tag{5}$$

5. Average Service Unavailability Index: This index measures the customer weighted unavailability of the system over the course of a year.

$$\text{ASUI} = \frac{\text{Customer hours of unavailable service}}{\text{Customer hours demanded}} \tag{6}$$

6. Energy Not Supplied: This index measures the total energy not supplied by the system over the course of a year.

$$\text{ENS} = \text{Total energy not supplied by the system} \tag{7}$$

7. Average Energy Not Supplied: This index measures the average customer total energy not supplied over the course of a year.

$$\text{AENS} = \frac{\text{Total energy not supplied by the system}}{\text{Total number of customer served}} \tag{8}$$

Load node indices are also considered including the failure rate λ_i, unavailability U_i, mean time to repair r_i, at node i. Furthermore, other load point indices related with steady-state and dynamic behavior are addressed. More details about the simulation model and its evaluation are presented in (Issicaba et al., 2011).

6. Numerical results

This section presents quantitative and qualitative results for the application of the agent-based architecture in a modified edition of the test system RBTS-BUS2-F1 (Allan et al., 1991). Fig. 10 pictures a single line diagram for this system as well as the grid segments for which the block agents are assigned. These assignments were derived from the basic grid protection segmentation given by the breaker positioning.

The design of this system follows general utility principles and practices regarding topology, ratings and load levels (Billinton & Jonnavithula, 1996). Network parameters and additional data are introduced in (Issicaba et al., 2011). Verification and validation of basic performance indices for this system, disregarding any agency, are shown in (Issicaba et al., 2011) as well.

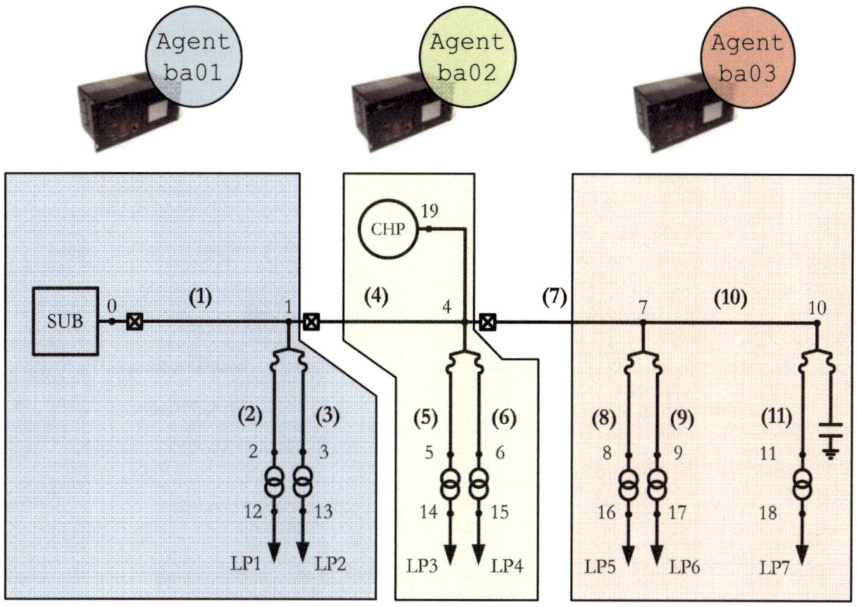

Fig. 10. Distribution network under operation the agent-based architecture support.

The electrical steady-state and dynamic behavior of this system were validated using the power system analysis software EUROSTAG (version 4.3) (GDFSUEZ & RTE, 2004).

Note that the applicability of plans of action depend upon the grid under control. For instance, it is not possible to support voltage control whether equipments to control voltage are not available. Therefore, for the sake of clarity and consistency, the test system was evaluated considering that only the plan `@DGislanded_operation_plan04` and its sub-plans were allowed. Hence, simulation with and without `block` agent were performed. The coefficient of variation (β) minimum value (Rubinstein & Kroese, 2008) was narrowed to 5% and all simulations were subjected to the same seed sequence of events to guarantee the comparison validity. Comparative results are presented in Table 1.

Index	without agents		with agents	
	Value	β (%)	Value	β (%)
SAIFI (interruptions/cust./yr)	0.134205121	1.84714948	0.105423358	1.84002804
SAIDI (h/cust./yr)	3.628097573	4.80371101	3.480572107	4.99916932
CAIDI (h/interruptions)	27.033972705	-	33.015189308	
ASAI	0.999584696	0.00199583	0.999601583	0.00199255
ASUI	0.000415304	4.80371101	0.000398417	4.99916932
ENS (MWh)	8.388050112	3.11734276	8.082481157	3.21803404
AENS (MWh/cust)	0.012865108	3.11734276	0.012396443	3.21803404
Number of simulated years: 12365				

Table 1. Comparative evaluation of grid performance indices

The outcomes show an improvement in quality of service. The most affected index was the SAIFI which reduced 21.45%. This means that an average customer should expect 21.45% less sustained service interruptions during a year due to the agent-based architecture. This was expected since the plan `@DGislanded_operation_plan04` is assigned to the goal *minimize*

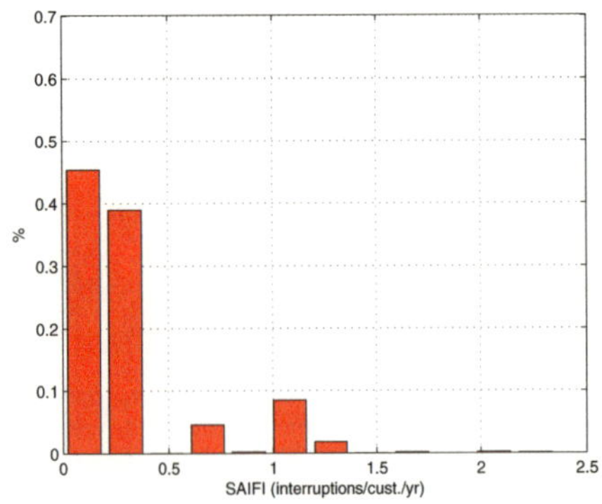

(a) without agents

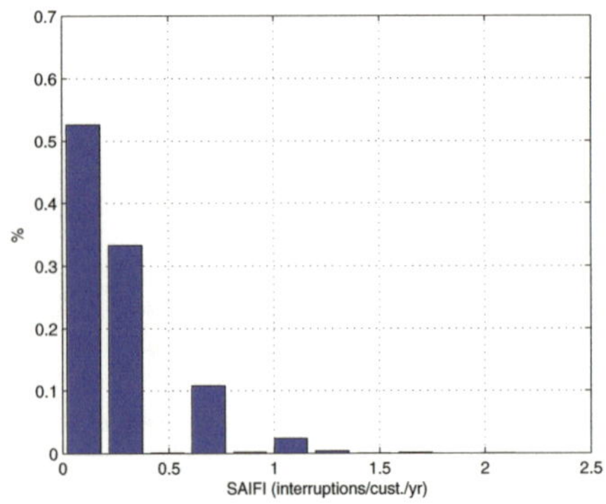

(b) with agents

Fig. 11. Estimated SAIFI probability distributions.

Node number	without agents			with agents		
	λ	U	r	λ	U	r
12	0.1182	3.7543	3.2633	0.1182	3.7543	3.2633
13	0.1111	3.5390	3.3688	0.1111	3.5390	3.3688
14	**0.1651**	3.5701	3.2666	**0.0761**	3.1140	2.9519
15	**0.1562**	3.7508	3.4494	**0.0672**	3.2963	3.1502
16	0.2137	3.9129	3.5053	0.2145	3.9152	3.5072
17	0.2152	3.6364	3.3204	0.2161	3.6388	3.3224
18	0.2508	4.0187	3.4918	0.2517	4.0211	3.4935
19	**0.1474**	0.7432	0.6927	**0.0584**	0.2871	0.2778

Table 2. Comparative evaluation of load point performance indices

interruptions (see Fig. 5), and infer directly in the grid protection rules aiming at serving the customers through DG islanded operation when necessary.

Since time-dependencies are explicitly represented in the combined discrete-continuous simulation model, the performance index histograms to the distribution grid operation can be rigorously derived. Fig. 11 depicts an histogram of the SAIFI values obtained during the 12365 year simulation (samples). Observe how the actual impact of the agent-based architecture can be enlightened by the index histograms. Due to the agent support, SAIFI values equal or superior to 1 interruption/customr/yr became rarer events and, depending on the quality of service regulation, this may avoid penalties to the utility. Finally, load point performance indices are also shown in Table 2. Nodes 12 and 13 (from block 01) have the same performance indices since they are not affected by the DG islanded operation plans. On the other hand, the performance indices at nodes 14, 15 and 19 (block 02) have improved significantly due to the proximity with the DG and the `ba02`'s planning. In particular, these nodes became more reliable and, consequently, more attractive to the connection of new customers/industries and DGs. Moreover, nodes 16, 17 and 18 kept almost the same indices with slightly differences. Observe that the reduction in customer interruptions is caused by the increase in successful DG islanding processes. Therefore, a larger amount of information about the system electrical/electromechanical dynamic behavior is produced, supporting the establishment of new agent plans regarding control schemes such as load shedding.

7. Conclusion and final remarks

Implementing agent-based systems is an interesting task that involves a lot of correlated areas within the computation and artificial intelligence sciences, as well as specific expertise linked to the application area. In order to reach and implement some fundamental aspects about agent-based systems, it is necessary to use some computational mechanisms that will allow the embodiment of autonomy, intelligence and mobility, among other characteristics, during the agent processing. Since the 1990s, several features have been introduced into the computation area, perhaps affected by the growth of the World Wide Web (www) and the rapid rise of e-Commerce, which enabled the construction of agent-based systems.

Based on these features, it is clear that there is much activity in this area around the world. Several middlewares, platforms, frameworks and environments have appeared in the last years in order to help programmers developing multi-agent systems. In the JAVA world, it is mandatory to highlight first the combination of JAVA, JASON and AgentSpeak as a successful way to code multi-agent systems, and second some advances in the pre-conceptual architectural phase to modeling agent-based systems. Undoubtedly, methodologies such as Prometheus are essential to model any agent-based system.

From the technological front, one of the challenges into smart grid concepts applied to distribution grid automation is to monitor, control, and coordinate the electrical grid efficiently with intelligence. Certainly, agent-based technology may be considered as an efficient way to deal with these challenges, providing flexible and autonomous software systems to solve a growing number of complex problems. This chapter has introduced agent-based technology through the two perspectives: simulation and modeling, and grid automation. Therefore, a new agent architecture was presented, where agent plans can be tested through the reliability studies, highlighting the benefits of some smart control solutions into distribution grids.

8. Acknowledgements

This work was supported by the Foundation for Science and Technology (FCT) – ref. SFRH/BD/43049/2008, the MIT Portugal Program on Sustainable Energy Systems, the *Fundo de Apoio à Inovação* within the framework of Project REIVE (Smart Grids with Electric Vehicles), the FCT Project Microgrids+EV: Identification of Control and Management Strategies for Microgrids with Plugged-in Electric Vehicles – ref. PTDC/EEA-EEL/103546/2008, and the Institute for Systems and Computer Engineering of Porto (INESC Porto).

9. Nomenclature

AC	Alternating Current
AM/FM	Automated Mapping Facility Management
BDI	Belief-Desire-Intention
CIS	Customer Information System
CT	Current Transformer
DA	Distribution Automation
DC	Direct Current
DER	Distributed Energy Resources
DG	Distributed Generation

DMS	Distribution Management System
EV	Electric Vehicle
FPI	Fault Passage Indicator
GIS	Geographical Information System
IED	Intelligent Electronic Device
RTU	Remote Terminal Unit
SA	Substation Automation
SCADA	Supervisory Control and Data Acquisition
TCM	Trouble Call Management System
VT	Voltage Transformer

10. References

Allan, R. N., Billinton, R., Sjarief, I., Goel, L. & So, K. S. (1991). A reliability test system for educational purposes-basic distribution system data and results, *IEEE Transactions on Power Systems* 6(2): 813–820.

Amin, M. (2001). Toward self-healing energy infrastructure systems, *IEEE Computer Applications in Power* 14(1): 20–28.

Baxevanos, I. S. & Labridis, D. P. (2007). Implementing multiagent systems technology for power distribution network control and protection management, *IEEE Transactions on Power Delivery* 22(1): 433–443.

Billinton, R. & Jonnavithula, S. (1996). A test system for teaching overall power system reliability assessment, *IEEE Transactions on Power Systems* 11(4): 1670–1676.

Billinton, R. & Li, W. (1994). *Reliability Assessment of Electrical Power Systems Using Monte Carlo Methods*, Plenum Press, Springer, New York.

Billinton, R. & Wang, P. (1999). Teaching distribution system reliability evaluation using monte carlo simulation, *IEEE Transactions on Power Systems* 14(2): 397–403.

Bordini, R. H., Hübner, J. F. & Wooldridge, M. (2007). *Programming Multi-Agent Systems in AgentSpeak using Jason*, John Wiley & Sons.

Bratman, M. E., Israel, D. J. & Pollack, M. E. (1988). Plans and resource-bounded practical reasoning, *Computational Intelligence* 4(4): 349–355.

Brown, R. E. (2002). *Electric Power Distribution Reliability*, Marcel Dekker, Inc., New York.

Cunha, L., Reis, J. & Peças, A. (2008). Inovgrid project - distribution network evolution as a decisive answer to new electrical sector challenges, *IET Seminar Digests* .

Davidson, E. M. & McArthur, S. D. J. (2007). Exploiting multi-agent system technology within an autonomous regional active network management system, *Proceedings of the 14th International Conference on Intelligent Systems Application to Power Systems.*

Dimeas, A. L. & Hatziargyriou, D. (2005). Operation of a multiagent system for microgrid control, *IEEE Transactions on Power Systems* 20(3): 1447–1455.

EPRI (2005). The intelligrid consortium research and development plan 2005-2007, *Technical report*.

ETP, S. G. (2008). Advisory council for the technology platform for europe's electricity networks of the future, european technology platform smartgrids: Strategic deployment document for europe's electricity networks of the future, *Technical report*, European Comission. Draft Version.

Flanagan, M. T. (2011). Michael thomas flanagan's java scientific library (open source), *http://www.ee.ucl.ac.uk/ mflanaga/java/index.html* .

GDFSUEZ & RTE (2004). Tractebel engineering gdf suez and rte, eurostag, *http://www.eurostag.be* .

Hopkinson, K., Wang, X., Giovanini, R., Thorp, J., Birman, K. & Coury, D. (2006). Epochs: a platform for agent-based electric power and communication simulation built from commercial off-the-shelf components, *IEEE Transactions on Power Systems* 21(2): 548–558.

Hossack, J. A., Menal, J., McArthur, S. D. J. & McDonald, J. R. (2003). A multiagent architecture for protection engineering diagnostic assistance, *IEEE Transactions on Power Systems* 18(2): 639–647.

IEEEP2030 (2011). Ieee guide for smart grid interoperability of energy technology and information technology operation with the electric power system (eps), end-use applications, and loads, *IEEE Standards Coordinating Committee 21* .

Issicaba, D., Gil, N. J. & Lopes, J. A. P. (2010). Islanding operation of active distribution grids using an agent-based architecture, *Proceedings of the Innovative Smart Grid Technologies Conference Europe (ISGT Europe)*, Stockholm, Sweden.

Issicaba, D., Rosa, M. A. & Lopes, J. A. P. (2011). Distribution systems performance evaluation considering islanded operation, *Proceedings of the Power System Computation Conference*, Stockholm, Sweden.

Kundur, P. (1993). *Power Systems Stability and Control*, McGraw-Hill, Inc.

Law, A. M. (2007). *Simulation Modeling & Analysis*, McGraw-Hill Series in Industrial Engineering and Management Science, fourth edn, McGraw-Hill.

Liu, D. & Antsaklis, P. J. (eds) (2009). *The Art of Agent-Oriented Modeling*, L. S. Sterling and K. Taveter, The MIT Press, Cambridge, Massachusetts.

Machowski, J., Bialek, J. W. & Bumby, J. R. (2008). *Power Systems Dynamics: Stabiltity and Control*, 2nd edn, John Wiley & Sons.

Manzoni, A. (2005). *Development of an Object-Oriented Computation System for Power Systems: Fast Simulation and Voltage Stability Application*, PhD thesis, COPPE/RJ, (in Portuguese).

McArthur, S. D. J., Davidson, E. M., Catterson, V. M., Dimeas, A. L., Hatziargyriou, N. D., Ponci, F. & Funabashi, T. (2007). Multi-agent systems for power engineering applications - part i: Concepts, approaches, and technical challenges, *IEEE Transactions on Power Systems* 22(4): 1743–1752.

Nagata, T. & Sasaki, H. (2002). A multi-agent approach to power system restoration, *IEEE Transactions on Power Systems* 17(2): 457–462.

Nagata, T., Tao, Y., Kimura, K., Sasaki, H. & Fujita, H. (2004). A multi-agent approach to distribution system restoration, *Proceedings of the 47th Midwest Symposium on Circuits and Systems*, Vol. 2.

Nagata, T., Tao, Y., Sasaki, H. & Fujita, H. (2003a). A multiagent approach to distribution system restoration, *Proceedings of the IEEE Power Engineering Society General Meeting*, Vol. 2.

Nagata, T., Tao, Y., Sasaki, H. & Fujita, H. (2003b). A multiagent approach to distribution system restoration, *IEEE Power Engineering Society General Meeting* 2: 655–660.

NETL (2007). National energy technology laboratory, a system view of the modern grid (appendix a1: Self-heals), *Technical report*, U.S. Department of Energy.

Northcote-Green, J. & Wilson, R. G. (2006). *Control and Automation of Electrical Power Distribution Systems*, CRC Press.

Pagdgham, L. & Winikoff, M. (2007). *Developing Intelligent agents systems – A practical guide*, John Wiley & Sons.

Rehtanz, C. (2003). *Autonomous Systems and Intelligent Agents in Power System Control and Operation*, Springer.

Rosa, M. A., da Silva, A. M. L., Miranda, V., Matos, M. & Sheblé, G. (2009). Intelligent agent-based environment to coordinate maintenance schedule discussions, *International Symposium on Intelligent Systems Applications to Power Systems.*

Rosa, M. A., Miranda, V., Carvalho, L. & da Siva, A. M. L. (2010). Modern computing environment for power system reliability assessment, *Proceedings of the Probabilistic Methods Applied to Power Sytems*, Singapore.

Rubinstein, R. Y. & Kroese, D. P. (2008). *Simulation and the Monte Carlo Method*, Wiley's Series in Probability and Statistics, 2nd edn, John Wiley & Sons, Inc, New Jersey.

Russell, S. & Norvig, P. (2002). *Artificial Intelligence: A Modern Approach*, 2nd edn, Prentice Hall.

Solanki, J. M., Khushalani, S. & Schulz, N. N. (2007). A multi-agent solution to distribution systems restoration, *IEEE Transactions on Power Systems* 22(3): 1026–1034.

Subcommittee, P. M. (1979). Ieee reliability test system, *IEEE Transactions on Power Apparatus and Systems* 98(6): 2047–2054.

2

Conflict Resolution in Resource Federation with Intelligent Agent Negotiation

Wai-Khuen Cheng[1] and Huah-Yong Chan[2]
[1]*Department of Computer Science, Universiti Tunku Abdul Rahman*
[2]*School of Computer Sciences, Universiti Sains Malaysia*
Malaysia

1. Introduction

Resource federation in grid computing (Foster et al., 1999, 2001) still requires extensively intervention of resource administrator which is time and cost consuming. This limitation leads to the idea of applying the autonomous intelligent agent to ease the process of resource federation (Foster et al., 2004). The participation and contribution of resources are based on a set of rules and regulations, namely local administrative policies. The local administrative policies can be further detailed into accounting policy, access control policy, resource usage policy and more (Foster et al., 2001). In this study, resource usage policy (as shown in Fig. 1) specifies the requirements and limits on particular resources during resource federation between various participants. A consensus among the participants is achieved through a bargaining mechanism, which aims at maximizing the satisfaction level during policy negotiation. The policy negotiation involves the satisfaction of policy criteria.

Policy in Level 1

Compute_Node() ← QualityOfService() + Accounting()
Comments : ***Compute node selection is based on QoS and charge of provided resource.***

Policy in Level 2

QualityOfService() ← Computation() + Bandwidth() + FaultRecovery()
Comments : ***The QoS requires the specification of compute power, network bandwidth and fault recovery mechanism.***

Accounting() ← TokenPerHour() + Availability()
Comments : ***The accounting requires cost per hour over resource duration.***

Policy in Level 3

Computation() ← ProcessorArch() + Speed_GFlops()
Comments : ***The resource compute power mentions about the processor architecture and speed in GFlops.***

Bandwidth() ← NetworkType() + NetworkSpeed()
Comments : ***The network bandwidth mentions about the type of network and speed.***

Fig. 1. Resource usage policies with various policy criteria.

Those criteria listed out the terms and conditions during resource federation, such as the resources to be shared, the participants who are allowed to utilize the resources, and also restrictions of sharing. Policy criteria can utilize a full range of qualitative and quantitative criterion. The matching of criteria between two participants is a complicated process because various types of criteria need to be fulfilled simultaneously. Both participants may not compromise at the beginning of matching, thus, a method to further increase the matching rate is needed. The common approaches, namely Constraint Satisfaction Problem (CSP) (Tsang, 1993) and Multi-Criteria Analysis (MCA) (Cheng et al., 2010), are studied to solve this problem.

CSP (Tsang, 1993) is a problem composed of a finite set of variables. Each of the variables is associated with a finite domain, and a set of constraints that restricted the values the variables can simultaneously take. The task of CSP is to assign a value to each variable satisfying all the constraints. MCA (Cheng et al., 2010) means there are multiple criteria related to a particular decision waiting for a result determination. A single criterion matching emphasizes the optimizing of the corresponding criterion value. However, multi-criteria matching which could achieve the optimal solution for all related criteria is rare and impractical because the complexity is high. As a result, a solution to compromise the satisfaction level in order to generate optimal solution is more preferable. The optimal solution may not satisfy the greatest value in all criteria but the solution is confirmed to be the best combination with highest utility scoring value.

According to the empirical result, maximize the compromise level for both participants may not promise a success in negotiation. Effort is spent to generate a mutual acceptance between participants but failed. Looking for another resource (participant) may not worth to perform since no guarantee for a success. Certain level of toleration in satisfaction can be applied but a comparative model for toleration (how to compensate equally with the amount of toleration) is still an open issue. Conventional automated negotiation approaches mainly solved arguments between two participants with conflict avoidance behaviour. Both participants will preferably withdraw from the negotiation process and looking for others resources when criteria cannot be satisfied. They assume terminating the relationship is a win-win situation since the resource pool has more choices.

As shown in Fig. 2, resource federation in grid environment can be mainly categorized into manual and automated approaches. Manual approaches requires human administrator to perform sequential resource matching. If three different types of resources are required in a resource federation scenario, then the human administrator may need to select and match the corresponding requirements from the available resource pools sequentially. This is believed to be time and cost consuming. Due to the limitation of manual approach, several automated approaches have been introduced. Among various types of implementation techniques, the intelligent agent is the famous adoption in automated approaches. This is due to the agent's features such as autonomous, flexibility and reactive to environment. These features are discussed and validated in papers (Cheng et al., 2005, 2006, 2010). The automated approaches can further be divided into non-negotiation (Xie & Qi, 2006; Russell et al., 2004) and negotiation techniques (Cheng et al., 2010; Ströbel & Weinhardt, 2003). Non-negotiation techniques are direct resource matchmaking without spaces of bargain. In contrast to non-negotiation techniques, negotiation techniques provide a bargaining mechanism to counter-offer between two agents before striking the final deal.

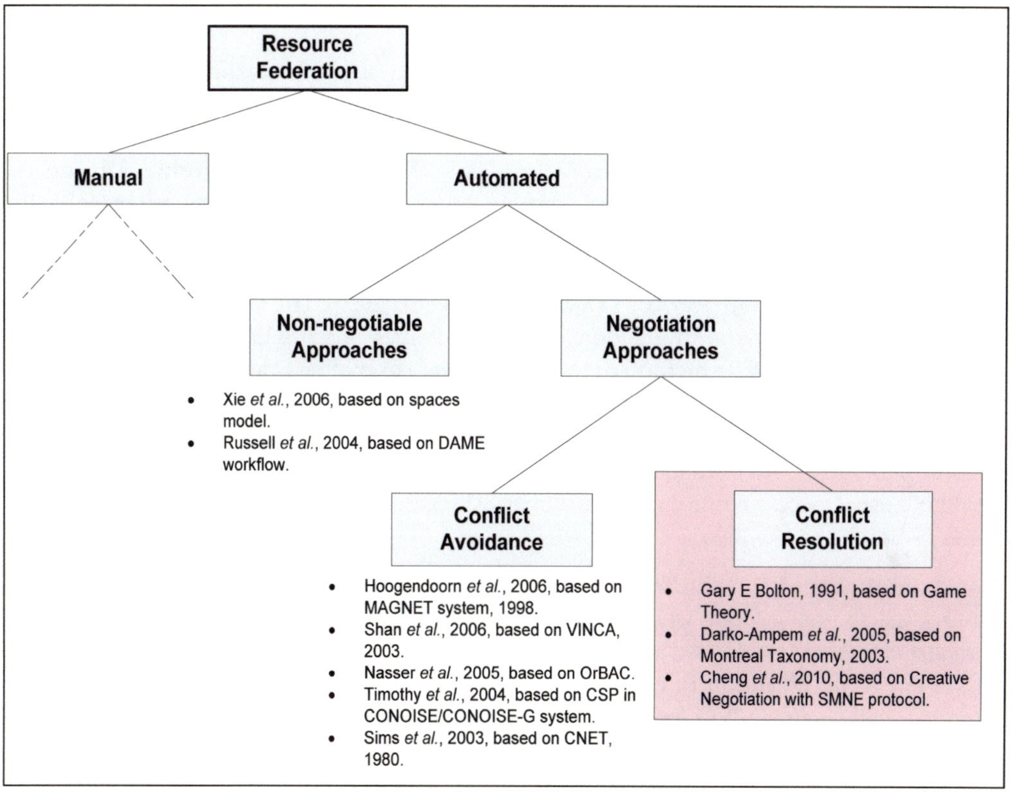

Fig. 2. Categorization of agent negotiation in resource federation.

The purpose of our study is to investigate and propose a conflict resolution model for multi-agent negotiation during resource federation. In order to provide a comprehensive review of possible solutions in agents' conflict resolution, various types of sophisticated negotiation approaches (e.g. logrolling, bridging, brainstorming, expand the pie) are compared and discussed. A concept of Creative Negotiation (Billikopf, 2003) which yet to be applied in automated conflict resolution with intelligent agent is proposed in this paper. Several technical challenges need to be reviewed during different stages of multi-agent negotiation implementation. The adoption of a Select, Match, Negotiate and Expand (SMNE) protocol (Cheng et al., 2010) helps in illustrating the overall framework of agent negotiation.

2. Resource federation

Resource federation in grid emphasizes a flexible and secure resource sharing mechanism. Higher flexibility of resource policy negotiation and more secure resource accessibility increase the confidence of participants in coordinating their resources. However, the mentioned characteristics bring several challenges during user authentication and authorization, resource access and resource matchmaking. Our research focuses on how to provide a scalable resource federation framework with automated policy negotiation under the domain of resource matchmaking. A comprehensive analysis of the state-of-the-art of resource federation framework is conducted to solve the problem above.

2.1 Why automate the resource federation?

The early work in grid resource federation is to manually select the participants for a Virtual Organization (VO) by VO initiator (administrator). VO is formed among the geographically dispersed participants in order to share their resources. The participant selection process has been improved with the aid of electronic media such as e-mail and e-forum. During the selection, the resource administrators play an important role during the communication since they are responsible in defining the resource usage policies. From various participant selection approaches, the most widespread implementation method is called Virtual Organization Membership Service (VOMS) (Alfieri et al., 2005). The VOMS approach owns a database which contains authorization data that defines specific capabilities and general roles for specific users. The method of proxy-certificate exchange is applied for user identity authentication and job submission during resource federation. The manual participant selection process in VOMS only solves the simple authorization problem. In a large scale resource federation environment, this method is not sufficient since a more challenging problem exists - access control over resources. The access control over resources is defined by the resource usage policies.

The administrators define the access control on each resource in corresponding policy. The resource usage policies help in defining the terms and conditions for resource sharing in a more structural and organized manner. On the other hand, when the VO initiator notifies the system of his intention to create a VO, the VO initiator will impose several resource usage policies (namely VO policies) to specify the requirements of different types of resources. The matchmaking between local administrative policies and VO policies can be implemented with different approaches. The initial common approach depends heavily on the intervention of human administrators. The administrators perform sequential policies matching in order to determine the qualified VO participants. A VO is established after both, local administrator and VO administrator, agreed upon the resource usage policies. This manual approach allows the administrator to be aware of each policy criterion and also assure the most preferable participants are chosen based on administrator perspective. However, as the complexity of policies increase due to the higher flexibility of policy criteria nowadays, the manual approach is become impractical. The limitations of manual policy matching are summarized below:

- Policies are difficult to search, organize and manage because the policy criteria is complicated and overloaded,
- Manual policy matching tends to be unsuccessful and requires repeatable matching because administrators find difficulty in considering all the policies synchronously,
- Lack of global consideration of resource utility since administrators only aware on frequent access policies,
- Manual approach increases the time and the cost in management because more effort are needed for human decision-making,
- Human administrator is unable to entertain requests in 24/7 (24 hours a day, 7 days a week).

Due to the limitations of manual approach in resource federation, such as overloaded policy management, lower resource satisfaction and optimization, time and effort consuming, several automated approaches are introduced, namely Globus Resource Allocation Manager

(GRAM) (Czajkowski et al., 1998) and Condor ((Litzkow et al., 1998). Both methods embedded with heuristic decision-making ability during resource selection. Major routine and trivial administrator workloads such as certificate validation and monitor resource availability have been automated to simplify the selection process. For example, in Condor, a ClassAd mechanism (Raman et al., 1998, 2003) was applied to match arbitrary resource requests with available resource offers. Several components like ClassAd specification, advertising protocol, matchmaking algorithm, matchmaking protocol and claiming protocol are designed in the matchmaking framework. The matchmaker tries to satisfy respective resource provider advertisements constraint (policy terms or criteria) and inform the relevant entities match. Furthermore, a sorted ranking mechanism is applied when multiple resources fulfilled the requirements.

Even though the automated approaches have addressed several limitations of manual approaches, room for improvement still exist. Firstly, resource administrator is required to define policies in a structural format, in order to make those policies more manageable. Secondly, a multi-criteria selection method is needed since different resource administrators may emphasize different criteria on the same kind of resource. Sometimes VO administrator is required to deal with imperfect knowledge on certain criteria during resource selection. The quality of decision-making with automated approach is often being criticized. Thirdly, during resource selection and policy reconciliation, several constraints impose on the resources may hinder a successful federation because VO and local resource administrators have different set of policies (VO policy, for all VO participants to follow during federation; local administrative policy, to control the accessibility of local resource from VO participants). An approach to address proper resource semantics for the definition of the usage and accessibility of resources is needed, such as the research works mentioned in Czajkowski et al., 2004; Dave, 2004; Djordjevic & Dimitrakos, 2004; Moses, 2005 and Naqvi & Mori, 2009.

2.2 Automated approaches in resource federation

As shown in the Fig. 2, automated approaches are categorized into non-negotiation and negotiation methods. Non-negotiation method can perform faster than negotiation method during policy matching. This is because non-negotiation method does not require bargaining on the policy criteria. It just allows the administrator to either accept or reject the listed policies. This method is obviously faster and cheaper because less processing is needed. Besides that, since bargaining is not applied into non-negotiation methods, the policy criteria are easier to be organized. For example, during negotiation process, the upper and lower bound of the criteria value are defined in a policy. This allows participants to compromise according to situation. A function to decide the exact bargaining value for each criterion is incorporated. However, non-negotiation methods can save this effort.

The federation of grid resources using non-negotiation methods included Russell et al., 2004 (a mechanism for securely sharing service instances by using grid computing in a diagnostics environment), Xie & Qi, 2006 (proposed a space-based coordination model to establish diverse VOs with special sharing policies), Network Queuing Environment (a batch submission system allowed users to create and submit job with specific resource requests and monitor the progress) (Cray Inc., 1997), Portable Batch System (provided scheduling execution and routing of batch jobs between different resources) (Bayucan et al.,

1999) and Load Sharing Facility (enabled system to redistribute workload among the hosts to improve performance and accessibility to remote resources) (Zhou et al., 1993). Some of these non-negotiation methods provide automated resource discovery and matching mechanism. However, the inflexibility of policy enforcement with static rules prohibits these methods to be applied in recent grid resource federation.

Due to the weaknesses of non-negotiation method, several negotiation methods have been studied. A flexible and robust negotiation method is proposed to solve the limitations of non-negotiation method. The robustness of negotiation addresses the issue of policy reconciliation between parties. The negotiation method must provide fault recovery mechanism during resource federation. For instance, appropriate solution is taken to avoid operation failures in a VO, such as dynamic join and leave for participants, and routine occurrence of resource failures in a large VO.

Legion grid architecture (Grimsaw & Wulf, 1996) provides an object-based approach for resource federation. A simple but generic scheduler defines the access and usage through diverse policies. Legion has highlighted the importance to counteract the fault tolerance during resource federation. According to Grimsaw and Wulh (Grimsaw & Wulf, 1996), writing fault tolerant distributed applications were difficult and error prone, thus, effort and risk in solving this problem must consider in the solution design. This shows the importance of robustness in distributed applications.

Reid G. Smith developed a contract net protocol (Smith, 1980) to specify problem-solving communication and control over the participants in a distributed problem solver. This protocol describes how resources can be distributed among a set of participants. However, no counter-offer and constraints relaxation are allowed in contract net protocol. Four important components of negotiation mechanism are discussed in paper Smith, 1980:

- A negotiation is a local process that did not involve centralized control,
- There is a two-way exchange of information during negotiation,
- Each negotiation participant evaluates the information from his own perspective,
- The final agreement of a bargaining is achieved by mutual selection.

Constraint Directed Negotiation (Sathi, 1990) represents the decision-making in negotiation as a solution to Constraint Satisfaction Problem (CSP). The task of CSP is to assign a value to each variable that satisfying all the constraints. Negotiation capability in CSP helps to improve the success rate of bargaining process. The constraint directed negotiation defines the constraints in qualitative mode only, but a complicated system like grid resource federation requires the policy criteria to be both qualitative and quantitative. Therefore, the applicability of constraint directed negotiation in distributed environment is arguable.

Web services-based standards within the context of the Open Grid Services Architecture (OGSA) (Foster et al., 2002) are among the famous adoption of grid technologies recently. The OGSA relies on a set of emerging web services (WS) specifications, such as Web Service Resource Framework (WSRF), Web Service Description Language (WSDL) and WS-Negotiation protocol, within the grid community. The web services with grid-connectivity are giving a name called grid services. Generally, a grid service use Simple Object Access Protocol (SOAP) or Representational State Transfer (REST)-style Extensible Markup Language (XML) enveloper with its own interface described by WSDL. A transaction between service requestor and service provider normally require the negotiability in order to increase the flexibility and efficiency of grid service discovery and matching. Hung et al. (Patrick et al., 2004) proposed the WS-Negotiation protocol to solve this problem. In WS-Negotiation framework, participants perform under provider-requestor relationship where both negotiate on a set of policy criteria. Either participant can determine to negotiate on selective criteria. Later, each participant will sort the criteria according to its significance before bargaining. In general, the WS-Negotiation contained three parts:

- Negotiation Message - which describes the format for messages exchanged between negotiation participants,
- Negotiation Protocol - which describes the mechanism and rules that negotiation participants should follow, and
- Decision-making - which is an internal and private decision process based on negotiation strategies.

In addition, WS-Negotiation also presented a Web Service Level Agreement (WSLA) which is the suggested model in SLA template. Andrieux et al., 2005 investigated the WS-Agreement and mentioned the importance to have a language and a protocol that publicizes what a service provider has to offer, in order to create agreements, as well as having a monitoring service. WS-Negotiation only provides a protocol for one-to-one single round negotiation. Therefore, an advanced version of WS-Agreement which allows multiple-round negotiations is proposed by Waeldrich et al., 2011. The proposed method helps in solving the iterative negotiation problem.

Other automated negotiation methods in the literature included Mobach et al., 2005 which used two-tier negotiation model in WS-Agreement to develop a one-to-many negotiation platform, Sadri et al., 2002 adopted logic-based approach and a shared language for agent communication and negotiation, Binmore & Vulkan, 1999 implemented game theory for automated negotiation, Kasbah electronic agent marketplace (Chavez et al., 1997) adopted CSP for electronic commerce application, Venugopal et al., 2008 proposed an alternate offers protocol for bilateral negotiation during resource reservation, Cheng et al., 2006 adopted artificial intelligence method and one-to-many negotiation framework for resource allocation, Rubinstein alternating protocol (Paurobally et al., 2005) supported one-to-one negotiation on a given policy and Xplore coordination platform (Andreoli & Castellani, 2001) used bi-colored negotiation graph to represent negotiation states.

Compare to manual and automated non-negotiation approaches, automated negotiation approaches have higher flexibility because disputes during policy matching are able to solve with constraints relaxation and bargaining methods. Negotiation approaches can increase participant's satisfaction because both VO and local administrators can determine and demand for requested SLA. Furthermore, VO and local administrators possibly explore some hidden information (space of negotiation) for conciliation in order to increase the success rate of negotiation.

However, from the negative perspective the automated negotiation approach applies indirect policy matching, thus it consumes more time and cost in policy criteria determination and negotiation. It also requires the administrator to derive and represent his preferences precisely, thus allows the automation of negotiation to proceed accurately. According to Foster et al., 2004, autonomous intelligent agents have been applied to reduce the intervention of resource administrators. They believed the deployment of agents as autonomous problem solvers which act flexibly in uncertain and dynamic environments such as grid will solve the above problems.

2.3 Why applied autonomous agent in negotiation

The basic functionalities of an intelligent agent included autonomous, reactive and goal-oriented. Intelligent agent has been deployed into the grid applications over the past few years. The adoption of intelligent agent into the grid domain is because the grid environments require autonomous and flexible behaviors whereas agent systems need a robust infrastructure to support its functionalities (Foster et al., 2004). Agents are often required to organize themselves into a collective manner and coordinate their actions in order to deliver certain tasks. This is in line with the purpose of VO construction in grid environment. Applying agent technology in resource federation has various benefits over the previous mentioned automated negotiation approaches. Firstly, autonomous agents are designed to have only partial control and knowledge regarding the environment. Agents can communicate and coordinate in order to achieve local and global resource optimization. Secondly, agents are more sophisticated in coordination, collaboration and negotiation through agent communication protocol. This enables the decomposition of complex resource federation problems into individual sub request or task and to be handled by corresponding autonomous agents. The integration between grid and agent will undoubtedly create new challenges in resource federation. Therefore, this paper will further analyze some possible challenges in the mentioned area.

2.3.1 Definition of agent negotiation

Negotiation occurs when somebody want to create something new that neither participant could do on his own, or a problem, conflict or dispute between the participants is required to be resolved (Roy et al., 2009). If two participants are willing to negotiate, they prefer to search for agreement rather than to argue openly. This statement is only valid if the participants expect to give and take. Both participants are required to modify or give in according to their previous proposals. However, the participants involved always face the dilemmas of honesty and truth in making concession. The honesty and truth determine how well a participant exposes and believes in others. This is an important consideration during automated negotiation.

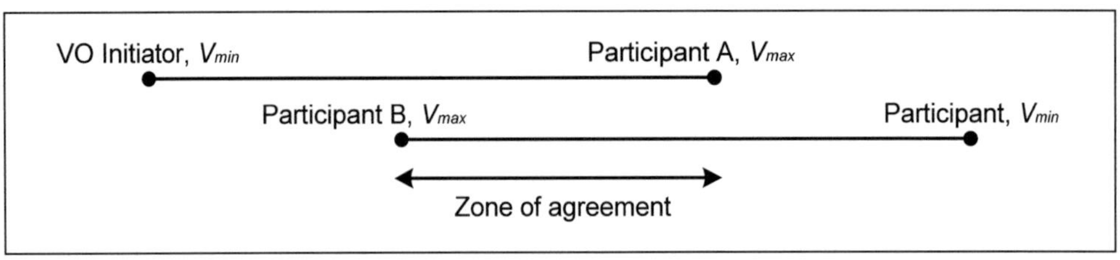

Fig. 3. Zone of agreement between two proposals.

An intelligent agent always explores a wider range of alternatives during negotiation. More alternatives (choices) constantly bring more chances in striking a deal. Normally, an upper limit, V_{max} and a lower limit, V_{min} for each criterion are set in filtering the alternatives. The filtering process is performed by referring to the existence of zone of agreement between two proposals. As shown in Fig. 3, a zone of agreement exists when the range of value between two participants are overlapped each other. Larger overlapping indicates higher chances in striking a deal during negotiation. Cheng et al., 2005 illustrated how to deal efficiently in a limited zone and find alternatives to satisfy both participants. Generally, a negotiation tactic is used to determine the value (within the upper and lower limits) to be offered in a particular criterion for the next counter-offer. A negotiation strategy is the determination of overall direction of bargaining tactics. Therefore, a negotiation strategy may contain multiple types of tactic for related criteria.

Negotiation tactics are short-term, adaptive moves designed to pursue higher-level negotiation strategies, which in turn provide stability, continuity and direction for tactical behaviors (Roy et al., 2009). Negotiation strategies are categorized into distributive and integrative. The distributive bargaining strategy applies a zero-sum game where individual gain is emphasized. The interests of negotiation are always opposed with opponent. On the other hand, the integrative bargaining strategy encourages a win-win negotiation or joint-gain. Since negotiators under this strategy have congruent interests and willing to cooperate, thus, the long-term relationship is introduced. Resource federation in grid is obviously a scenario of integrative bargaining. VO participants always search and perform the solutions that meet the goals and objectives of all. This idea is also applied in the proposed negotiation framework in this research.

However, integrative negotiation is difficult to solve compare to distributive negotiation due to several factors. For example, a terrible history of previous relationship worsens the cooperation magnitude. Some cognitive biases create perception and belief that a criterion is unable to be resolved in integrative mode. Besides, mixed-motive (mixture of distributive and integrative concerns on negotiation criteria) also resists the success of an integrative negotiation. Some participants are not willing to compromise with certain negotiation criteria. As a result, agreement will be terminated or never achieve with incomplete negotiation outcome. These challenges should be considered during the design of an integrative negotiation framework.

Perform automated negotiation between two agents involves several steps. Those steps included policy and requirement specifications, relationship building between participants with identification exchanged, information gathering with the opponent's needs, opponent's behavior and background analysis, bidding process, closing the deal, and lastly enforce the agreement. Applying autonomous agent in automated negotiation is the process of designing software agents to perform the mentioned functionalities on behalf of its owners. Challenges arise on how an agent can obtain the owner's preferences precisely. A hierarchical-based policy representation technique is adopted in the research to address this issue.

The conventional automated negotiation processes are separated into three phases, namely pre-negotiation, conduct of negotiation and post-negotiation. This is a slightly simplified version of the previous steps. The pre-negotiation is the start of the overall process. The preparation for bargaining such as determination of the criteria to be negotiated and assigning the appropriate values for the proposal are arranged. Second phase is making trade-off in order to satisfy both participants. Third phase is post-negotiation which involves negotiation resolution. The process of negotiation resolution included the agreement reconciliation and enforcement.

The main challenges of implementing automated negotiation with intelligent agents included:

- To securely delegate the agent with owner's authority,
- To clearly clarify different set of goals and expectations through negotiation tactics and strategies,
- To accurately represent owner's preferences into agent's belief,
- To cultivate positive relationships between agents by understanding different needs,
- To avoid any negative elements that could limit spaces of toleration, and
- To frequently explore beyond the obvious solution.

2.4 Conflict resolution in automated negotiation

Nowadays, the grid resource federation is more complicated compare to early solutions. However, the adoption of WS standards for latest OGSA provides arbitrary services for discovering and acquisition of heterogeneous resources easily. This requires higher flexibility in resource specification because the diverse policies used to control the access of resources become gradually complex. The conventional policy matching is unable to find a resource easily because the constraints imposed by different policies hinder the process. Due to this difficulty, a negotiation mechanism is needed. The resource federation which composes of multiple synchronous requests to different participants in a VO requested an agile and flexible yet organized method to solve the problem. Achieve satisfaction of different participants at the same time creates a challenge in grid resource federation. In this research, a Select, Match, Negotiate and Expand (SMNE) protocol is illustrated to depict the capability of conflict resolution of intelligent agent in a negotiation platform.

As mentioned earlier, the post-negotiation which involves conflict resolution and agreement enforcement plays an important role to ensure the success of a deal. Various types of distributed resources are attached with corresponding resource usage policies. Each policy will further detail into different criteria. Frequently, one common criterion in all policies may affect each others. For example, the allocation for several types of resources must be allocated in the same period. Conflicts between VO participants may happen when local administrative policies for each participant contradict each others. The resource federation is unable to proceed without a good mechanism to resolve the conflicts.

Compromising in either participant for the requested criteria can help in solving the disputes or conflicts. The compromise can either performed by the VO administrator or local administrator. This action is necessary to cultivate positive relationships between VO participants and also to avoid any negative elements that could limit spaces of toleration in the future. Besides, few circumstances may also require compromising from either participant:

- Limited participants during the resource federation because the possibility in locating the best participant is rare.
- Maximizes the satisfaction for both participants (VO and local administrators) in an integrative negotiation since local domain emphasizes on self-interested resource utilization while global resource utilization is important for a VO.

- Certain candidates are targeted as preferable VO participants during the resource federation, thus, compromising during policy reconciliation brings higher chances for a satisfied federation.

Policy reconciliation is categorized into conflict resolution technique in automated negotiation. Several conflict resolution techniques have been studied. Persuader system (Sycara, 1989) was developed to model adversarial conflict resolution in the domain of labor relations. Persuader system adopts both case-based reasoning (CBR) and multi-attribute utility theory (MAUT) to mediate conflicts between participants. Several intelligent agents negotiate on multi-criteria iteratively. A mediator agent is responsible to solve the conflicts between the company and union according to the social reasoning model. Iterative and incremental modification of agents' belief through counter-proposal is used to narrow down the differences between agents' goal. This system allows an agent to influence and change the opponent's belief incrementally. However, agent's belief may not be the same and could be unique in resource federation practically. A distributed system like grid computing has never centralized the configuration.

Besides applying reasoning ability in conflict resolution, several heuristic approaches have been proposed as well. For example, Mailler et al., 2004 applied hill climbing algorithm in Scalable Protocol for Anytime Mediation (SPAM) to identify the over-constrained criteria, subsequently, recommend an appropriate solution. Kraus proposed a strategic negotiation model for conflict resolution (Kraus, 2006) in multi-agent negotiation platform. The negotiation model offers sequencing and re-submission of new counter-offer when the offer rejected by either participant in the negotiation. Rahwan *et al.* proposed an automated negotiation with agent argumentation-based negotiation protocol (Rahwan et al., 2004). The proposed protocol allows agents to exchange additional information, or to "argue" and potentially influences others about its beliefs and mental attitudes during the bargaining. Furthermore, Barbuceanu and Lo, 2000 also developed a constraint optimization/relaxation and information exchanged negotiation engine to solve the conflicts in constraint satisfaction problems.

The Montreal taxonomy (Ströbel and Weinhardt, 2003) was used to classify and evaluate the negotiation protocols. In Ströbel and Weinhardt research, a rule-driven selection technique was proposed for conflicts resolution. A tie-breaking rule is applied to complement the resolution process. The tie-breaking rule will define how the selected conflicts are being resolved. Conflicts are forwarded and resolved by intelligent agents if resolution and tie-breaking rules unable to settle the problems. Conflicts in Montreal taxonomy are solved by using a fixed set of pre-defined rules. This is impractical for grid domain but the rules mentioned in the paper (Ströbel and Weinhardt, 2003) can refer as a guide in evaluating negotiation protocol.

Cheng et al. also presented a multi-agent negotiation framework with the comparison of performances between various machine learning methods (Cheng et al., 2005, 2006). In the proposed framework, the application of negotiation tactics and strategies during negotiation were demonstrated. Self-interested agents are applied to study the opponent's behavior in this framework. Local performance of the agent is emphasized to investigate the possibility in applying autonomous agent in grid environment. This framework is extended with more variety of agents, negotiation tactics and strategies, and also a comparison of the behavior of agents in distributive and integrative negotiation environments (Cheng et al., 2010). Several modules such as policy management and conflict resolution are added to examine the agent performances in the multi-agent negotiation platform.

In section 2.2, several automated negotiation techniques are listed. The mentioned techniques can be categorized either into conflict resolution techniques which can resolve the conflict and dispute between multiple participants, or conflict avoidance techniques which do not provide conflict resolution or mediation ability. For example, Globus (Czajkowski et al., 1998), Condor (Litzkow et al., 1998), Legion (Grimsaw & Wulf, 1996), contract net protocol (Smith, 1980) and logic-based approach (Sadri et al., 2002) are categorized under conflict avoidance techniques. These techniques either do not provide or only grant low level of conflict resolution ability. Compromising between participants will not exist in conflict avoidance techniques but more likely an automated direct policy matching will be applied. The conflict avoidance techniques are unable to cultivate positive relationships during resource federation between agents by understanding different needs. With comparison to game theory (Binmore & Vulkan, 1999), constraint relaxation protocol (Barbuceanu & Lo, 2000), argumentation-based approach (Rahwan et al., 2004), web service approach (Paurobally et al., 2005) and Montreal taxonomy approach (Ströbel & Weinhardt, 2003), these techniques provide a more powerful mechanism in handling the conflict and dispute during the conduct of negotiation. Nevertheless, several improvements in the above techniques are needed in order to provide better policy reconciliation in the problem of grid resource federation.

Besides the mentioned approaches, authors also study the possibility of integrating several well-known conflicts resolution techniques adopted in human negotiation. According to Roy et al., 2009, several applicable techniques are adopted in solving the conflict and dispute for integrative negotiation. These techniques are listed below.

i. Expanding the pie adds extra negotiation resources (e.g. policy criteria) to the current policy to achieve goals for both agents through integrative negotiation. This technique is useful since both agents always spend their effort in understanding other's needs. However, the resources to be expanded need to be determined carefully and not over-tiered than previous discussed policy. This method is chosen in the proposed SMNE protocol.
ii. Logroll, trade off among the policy criteria so that each participant alternately achieves highly preferred outcome on a particular criterion. Problem in this technique is how to decide who has the authority to start the selection of the preferred criterion. If both agents have the same highly preferred issue, then conflict may arise again.
iii. Applied nonspecific compensation allows an agent in obtaining its goals and pay off the other agent for accommodating its interests, where the compensation is not directly related to the substantive criteria being discussed. This technique requires the agent to know what is valuable to the other agent and how seriously the agent is inconvenienced due to the compromise. The distributive negotiation may happen once the compensation value is too demanding.
iv. Lowered the compliance costs, an agent achieves its goals meanwhile other values are minimized if the agent agrees to go along. This technique requires the knowledge of the other agent's actual needs and preferences. However, the solution spaces become restrictive because the criteria constraints are increased.

v. Generated bridge solution, is reformulation of the constraints and both agents disclose sufficient information to discover their interests and needs, thus, inventing alternatives that will satisfy both. However, the outcome of reformulation does not always remedy all concerns and both agents require compromising on the results. Furthermore, agents may also disclose irrelevant or private information without proper policy management.
vi. Other methods like brainstorming, nominal groups and surveys, will only be applied with the aid from a group of other agents. This requires extensive collaboration between the autonomous agents. This may not be applicable in resource federation because each agent in a VO is owned by different owners where each local administrator may vary in their opinions. Consensus may not easily achieve without a proper centralized management in the dynamic VO environment.

The application of intelligent agent allows the automation of negotiation process and exchange of messages in resource federation. The autonomous and flexible behaviors of the intelligent agent allow the owners to easily delegate his authority, preferences, goals and expectations onto the corresponding agent in an organized format. Several components are designed in order to develop an agent negotiation framework. For example, an automated negotiation protocol which defines actors, roles and negotiation phases; an agent communication protocol to define the agent's goals, strategies, tactics and criteria; a negotiation policy language to define normative understanding rules; and a negotiation policy taxonomy to identify different types of policy in negotiation environment.

From the findings of literature review, there is definitely no universal approach for automated negotiation which can solve all problems. Rather, a set of approaches have been proposed, each relied on different assumptions and constraints on the negotiation environment and the participants involved. An approach must be designed and evaluated from different perspectives (e.g. Montreal taxonomy) in order to verify the applicability as a problem solution. From the analysis, WS-based of resource description is suitable to be applied for user interaction. A flexible and robust negotiation protocol with conflict resolution capability is proposed to solve the grid resource federation. Several challenges such as policy representation, policy selection and autonomous negotiation are the important aspects considered in this chapter. An automated negotiation protocol with the adoption of intelligent agents is illustrated in the following section to solve the problem of resource federation.

3. Multi-agent negotiation platform

A comprehensive study and analysis on the available agent negotiation techniques has been carried out in the Section 2. An agent negotiation framework in grid resource federation with the consideration of challenges mentioned in Section 2.3.1 is proposed. A Java Agent Development Extension Framework (JADEX) (Braubach et al., 2006) is chosen as the agent development tool in this research. JADEX is applied because of the outstanding embedded reasoning engine - Belief-Desire-Intention (BDI) model (Rao & Georgeff, 1995). The concept of BDI is applied in performing decision making according to human mental attitudes. This concept is adopted by the intelligent agent since the agent is required to perform negotiation according to administrator preference. Besides BDI reasoning engine, JADEX also provides several middleware with standard protocol such as communication infrastructure and management facilities. For example, JADEX communication messages follow standard of

FIPA-ACL (Foundation for Intelligent Physical Agents - Agent Communication Language) (FIPA, 2002). FIPA promotes agent-based technology and the interoperability of its standards with other technologies. It provides the specifications for a standard agent language, ontology's structuring for the semantic content of messages and an abstract agency model.

The JADEX agents are written using two types of language - XML and Java. The XML is used to express the agent definition file (ADF). The content of an ADF consists of the agent's beliefs, goals, plans headers, triggering events and other agent instantiation properties. Each ADF binds with a corresponding logical structure written in Java language. Those logical structures define the actual behavior of an agent in handling the incoming action requests. JADEX provides a control centre to create multiple containers to hold different types of agents. In actual implementation, the main container resides on the local host. It runs the platform's Remote Method Invocation (RMI) server which allows agents from diverse containers on distributed platforms (resources) to utilize the RMI protocol to communicate. This can be used to simulate resource federation with distributed resources from different VOs.

In order to solve the problems of resource federation in a dynamic grid environment, a one-to-many resource selection protocol with one-to-one policy reconciliation using automated negotiation has been proposed. The proposed resource federation model is simulated and tested in a multi-agent platform using JADEX. Several machines are interconnected to represent the distributed grid topology. Each of the machines is deployed with one or more intelligent agents in representing diverse local site. Each site is owned by a different administrator with corresponding local resources. The accessibility of the resources is stated clearly in the resource usage policy which is drafted by the local administrator. Requirement and specification of resource sharing are listed in each policy criteria. A VO initiator will be randomly chosen from the list of agents in order to start the simulation of resource federation. Several scenarios are prepared to examine the proposed agent negotiation and conflict resolution protocol.

In this research, an automated negotiation framework with the integration of resource selection, policy negotiation and reconciliation, and multi-agent platform has been illustrated. According to several earlier experimental results (Cheng et al., 2005, 2006, 2010), the proposed integration method, namely Select, Match, Negotiate and Expand (SMNE) protocol, was well performed with different experimental data which included various quantitative and qualitative policy criteria. Therefore, further investigation is being conducted to examine the performance of the SMNE protocol.

3.1 Select, Match, Negotiate and Expand (SMNE) protocol

As shown in Fig. 4, the SMNE protocol mainly performs four major tasks:

i. Selection: The first task is the resource selection. A one-to-many policy evaluation is performed to differentiate policies from different participants. A list of potential participants is generated with the comparison of non-negotiable criteria from the policies for further one-to-one negotiation.
ii. Matching: The second task is to find out the negotiable criteria. Negotiable criteria are determined, ranked and weight by intelligent agent according to pre-assigned

administrator's preferences for further negotiation. A Multi-Criteria Analysis (MCA) method is applied during the policy evaluation.

iii. Negotiation: Iterative bargaining is performed based on the negotiable criteria (as stated in the resource usage policies) in achieving a mutual acceptance between the local and VO administrators. Several negotiation strategies and tactics can be applied at this stage to increase negotiation's outcome satisfaction.

iv. Expansion: This stage is only performed if negotiation has failed to reach a mutual acceptance. Compromise is needed in order to expand the spaces of negotiation. Some constraints are resolved to increase the satisfaction of both intelligent agents during a conflict or dispute.

For further explanation, the SMNE protocol is always initiated by the VO initiator (administrator) during the selection of participants. For automated resource federation with intelligent agents, the first challenge always faced by the developer is to securely delegate the agent with owner's authority. Security and trust management are adopted to authenticate the identity of VO participants and resolve different security conditions which apply to various resources. Several researches have been conducted, such as Djordjevic & Dimitrakos, 2004 and Naqvi & Mori, 2009 on security and trust management model. Grid security may not limit to the encryption of data during file transfer, tamper-proof to the intrusion by unauthorized intruders, delegation of authority for software communication, it also emphasizes on how to build up relationship in a trust management model. In an open grid environment, agents are requested to interact with other unfamiliar agents. Therefore, several security models such as public key infrastructure, access control list, role-based authentication and digital certificate authentication have been proposed and examined. These models may use centralized or decentralized repository to verify the identity of an agent. Either model can be adopted during the resource selection in the proposed SMNE protocol. Administrators feel more secure and comfortable in delegating their authority on the agents after applying the security model. This can avoid the unintended actions performed by the agents without a proper control with the model.

At the meantime of verification of the participant's identity, an administrator may also need to define criteria value, preferences, goals and other important parameters such as negotiation strategies, tactics and threshold values for bargaining. This will be the second challenge during the development process. As shown in Fig. 1, a hierarchical-based policy representation technique is adopted to represent the owner's preferences in resource usage policies. Owner can easily show his preferences on each criterion by using ranking and weighting mechanism. Rank Order Centroid (ROC), Analytic Hierarchy Process (AHP), or Simple Multi-attribute Rating Technique (SMART) can be applied to assign weight respectively (Cheng et al., 2010). Besides, a belief-based architecture is also adopted to represent the owner's preferences into the agent's belief. JADEX (Braubach et al., 2006) Agents incorporate the Belief-Desire-Intention (BDI) reasoning engine to mimic human actions and attitudes in decision making. Four types of goal (perform, achieve, query, and maintain) are introduced into the agent's lifecycle as the objectives to be achieved. Plans or actions are inter-correlated with corresponding goals to perform tasks being assigned by administrator. The BDI model allows the agent to represent different conditions and states easily.

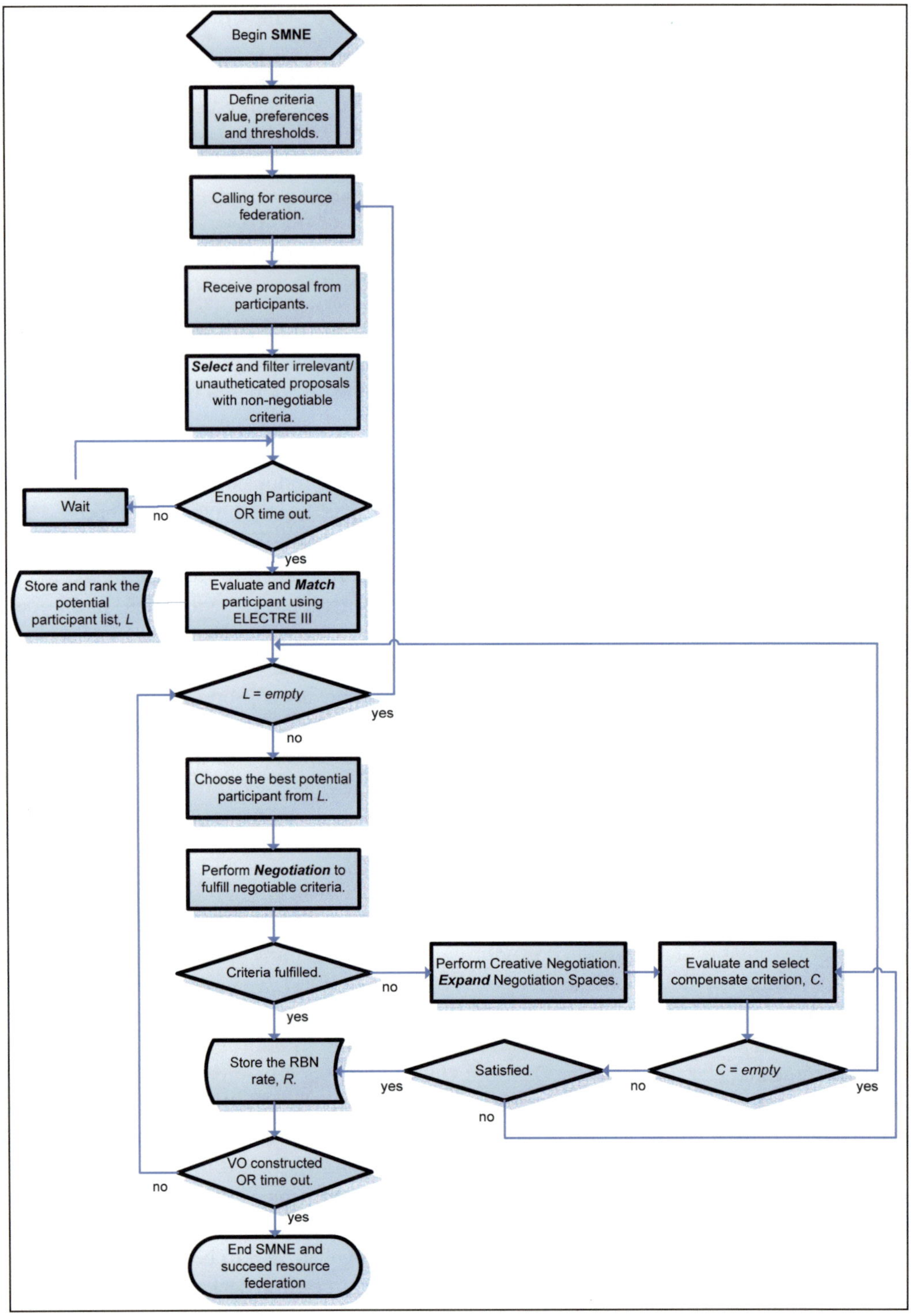

Fig. 4. Applying SMNE protocol in multi-agent conflict resolution (Cheng et al., 2010).

Furthermore, a negotiable criterion must have a range of valid choices which can be used in bargaining. A minimum acceptable value, V_{min}, is accompanied by another optimal maximum value, V_{max} in providing the choices (as shown in Fig. 3). Negotiation strategies and tactics are adopted to determine the value to be offered in each criterion during the offer and counter-offer process. The selection of negotiation strategy leads to the determination of overall direction of negotiation tactics. The common negotiation tactics included time-dependent, resource-dependent, behavior-dependent and relation-dependent (Cheng et al., 2005). Each tactic is modeled with a corresponding mathematical function to determine the next value during the counter-offer process. Meantime, a negotiation strategy is selected from the group of artificial intelligence method (e.g. fuzzy logic, neural network), heuristic method (e.g. reinforcement learning, aggressive, passive), relationship model (e.g. relation-based) and standard model (e.g. linearly increment, linearly decrement) (Cheng et al. 2006, 2010).

In SMNE protocol, a relationship model is adopted to determine the value to be offered during negotiation, namely Relation-Based Negotiation (RBN) strategy. The RBN strategy allows the agent to compromise according to the accumulated credibility from the past (Cheng et al. 2010). Better offer will be proposed in each attempt when both agents have more successful collaboration occurred before. The RBN is able to cultivate positive relationship between agents because agents more likely to share their resources in an integrative mode. Bad performance will be punished with credibility deduction where sincere collaboration will be rewarded with high credibility. This recalls the agents to always understand opponent's needs and avoid self-interested behavior.

After the selection of participants, the matching and evaluation of the proposals are performed by the agent. SMNE applies Multi-Criteria Analysis (MCA) method to evaluate and rank the received proposals. ELECTRE III (Cheng et al., 2010) is chosen after the comparison between various MCA and Constraint Satisfaction Problem (CSP) (Tsang, 1993) methods. Both methods are able to solve the problems pertaining to multi-criteria but MCA outperforms CSP in providing higher flexibility and modularity for administrator to characterize his preferences during proposal evaluation. Various methods can be applied in different modules (weighting, thresholding, utility aggregation) in order to fulfil different MCA requirements. Since MCA and CSP methods have the corresponding features to easily adopt administrator's preferences, authors also further compared the capability of MCA and CSP in performing criterion value compensation. The calculation of compensation needed was an attempt to quantify the credibility of opponent and also refer as a guide for the agent to perform next counter-offer in RBN. A comparison between RBN with conflict resolution and direct negotiate with new opponent during conflict is conducted in order to investigate the satisfaction of VO administrator in performing resource federation. The experiment is performed to examine the satisfaction of the proposed SMNE with the existence of different numbers of participants. The outcome can further explain the most suitable situation to apply conflict resolution in resource federation.

From the complexity aspect, MCA requires more computation power during pre-negotiation for weighting and thresholding. In this method, administrator also needs to provide more details on his preferences into the agent's belief. Meanwhile, CSP consumes more computation in the process of solution searching (conduct of negotiation) when the amount of criteria gets vast. The complexity of NP-complete in CSP urges for a better heuristic solution in policy negotiation. From negotiation aspect, CSP is more suitable for one-to-one negotiation compares to MCA. Most of the time, proposals from other participants will not be directly considered during CSP. The CSP is useful in performing a direct negotiation between two participants, where MCA takes a different approach to collect multiple concurrent proposals followed by an evaluation and ranking process. A one-to-many negotiation approach is adopted with MCA. Therefore, MCA is determined as more suitable solution for multi-criteria proposal evaluation.

Additionally, ELECTREE III applies pseudo-criteria with fuzzy outranking relation for proposal evaluation (Cheng et al., 2010). This feature allows ELECTRE III to deal with inaccurate, imprecise and uncertain data, which is applicable to the scenario of resource federation in dynamic grid environment. However, the tedious step of parameters configuration for threshold values, scoring and scaling functions requires further improvement.

From the generated list of participants, the proposal of highest order is chosen for further negotiation. Negotiation strategies and tactics are adopted at this stage for bargaining and trade-off. As mentioned earlier, RBN is adopted by SMNE protocol to cultivate positive relationship between agents. However, a bottleneck (conflict) may occur once both agents are unable to further compromise. As a solution, the agent can always seek for another participant from the list. But, this may not promise for a successful bargaining and possible lead to an exhaustion of time. In order to counteract this problem, the concept of Creative Negotiation (Billikopf, 2003) is proposed. Creative negotiation is only triggered in specific conditions. For example, once the agent discovers the opponent is unable to further provide a better offer (e.g. no or very small differences with the two continuous proposals from the same opponent), then one or more add-on criteria will be introduced into the bargaining to expand the negotiation spaces for conflict resolution (Cheng et al., 2010).

As listed in the Section 2.3.1, negotiation should always avoid any negative elements that could limit spaces of toleration. An autonomous agent should be design with the mechanism to frequently explore beyond the obvious solution. In SMNE protocol, agents always expand the spaces of negotiation (pie) with the concept of creative negotiation. A constraint is resolved with the compensation of additional criteria which may direct or indirect affect the unsatisfied criterion. For example, the VO administrator requests 1MB/sec of network transfer rate from a network service provider without the consideration of stability. Without the promise of stability, the downtime of network can seriously affect the performances. However, due to certain reasons the network service provider is unable to provide the requested speed but a different offer with additional consideration can be proposed. The network service provider can counter-offer the VO administrator with a minimum 512Kb/sec of network transfer rate and also a better quality of service with 99.9% of network availability during resource federation. The newly proposed criterion, namely network availability is generated to compensate the insufficient network transfer rate. An important concern is raised out through the bargaining and compensation process, thus, credibility can be awarded to the network service provider in rewarding the sincere integrative collaboration. Of course, a threshold value, T, is set to avoid the negotiation outcome deviate seriously from the initial requests. Further explanation of creative negotiation in SMNE protocol is discussed in the paper (Cheng et al., 2010).

4. Experimental results and discussion

A multi-agent negotiation platform is developed by using JADEX in order to simulate the grid resource federation. Several distributed grid topology is simulated with a group of interconnected machines. Agents are randomly deployed into each machine to represent the local administrators. Resource usage policies are also randomly assigned with different qualitative and quantitative values in order to represent diverse administrator's behavior in sharing their resources. Satisfaction and Time factors are tested in the experiments.

Satisfaction factor indicates the willingness of the agent to accept an offer during a negotiation. In the experiments, the differentiation between the final offered values from the opponent with agent's estimated (comfortable) value is calculated (1). Larger positive percentage indicates more comfortable or higher willingness of an agent to accept an offer, while 0% specifies the offer is in the expectation, and lower negative percentage indicates a higher level of dissatisfaction of an offer. In the experiments, the satisfaction of VO initiator (administrator) is captured because the VO initiator may need to coordinate and negotiate with different agents at the same time.

$$Statisfaction, \% = \frac{V_{offered} - V_{estimated}}{V_{estimated}} \tag{1}$$

Time factor shows how fast the VO initiator (agent) can achieve a mutual acceptance with an agent from the list of participants. Time calculated including proposals evaluation from a given number of participants and the overall negotiation process until a successful deal is achieved (2).

$$Time, t = t_{deal} - t_{start} \tag{2}$$

Experiments have repeated with different numbers of participants (agents), range from 10 - 200 participants. This intends to simulate a dynamic VO with different structures. Besides, two different types of method are compared, namely negotiation only method (NO) and conflict resolution method (CR). In negotiation method, if both agent failed to achieve a consensus, then the VO initiator will seek for another agent in the list. This action is repeated until the agent has successfully striking a deal. This method is also representing the conventoinal automated negotiation method. On the other hand, conflict resolution method will proceed with other solutions in resolving the conflict. As discussed in the proposed SMNE protocol, creative negotiation (Cheng et al., 2010) is applied in our experiments.

An experiment is conducted to investigate the satisfaction level between NO and CR with different numbers of participants. As mentioned earlier in Section 2.4, authors believed CR can outperform NO in staisfaction factor once the number of participants is small during the resource federation. Besides, the most suitable circumstances to apply CR compare to NO is also studied in order to provide a guide to VO administrator for future reference during participant selection. According to Fig. 5, experimental results show that:

- Agents achieve higher satisfaction with more participants in a VO.
- CR only outperforms NO when the number of participants is limited (<90 participants).

- CR can achieve better satisfaction when NO finds difficulty in striking a deal (number of participants = 20, 60, 140).
- None of the method can absolutely outperform the other when the number of participants is getting larger.

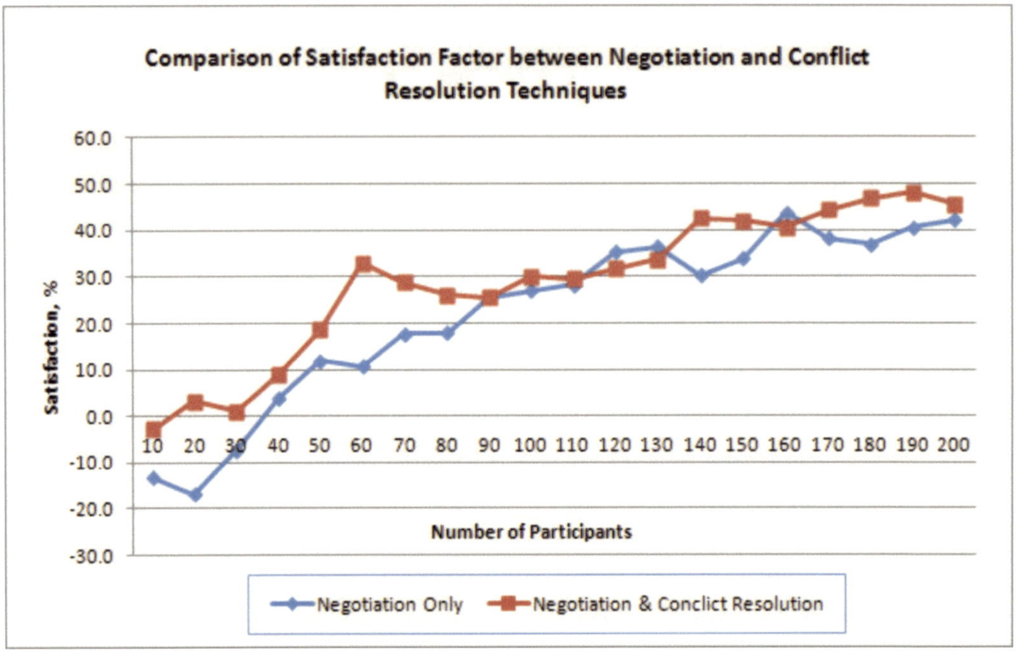

Fig. 5. The comparison of satisfaction factor in multi-agent negotiation between NO and CR.

With the same experiment setup, overall time for the proposals evaluation, negotiation until striking a deal has been captured. This experiment is performed to examine the capability of the NO and CR methods in striking a deal in reasonable time frame. Meanwhile, authors also intended to evaluate the additional time and effort spent in locating new participant under the NO method. Fig. 6 shows the following findings:

- A gradually increment of processing time for both methods, NO and CR.
- CR in average takes shorter time in striking a deal compare to NO.
- NO always takes longer time in striking a deal when most of the participants is unable to compromise (number of participants = 20, 60, 140).
- CR is a more stable and predictive model compare to NO.

As shown in both figures (Fig. 5 and Fig. 6), SMNE protocol is useful especially when the VO has limited participants. Level of satisfaction in SMNE protocol can be maintained meanwhile the conventional automated negotiation method is struggling for a successful deal with multiple participants when none of them can further compromise. As a conclusion, a faster and time-predictable method is performed by SMNE protocol. This has proved the previous arguments on the applicability of conflict resolution method in automated agent negotiation as stated in Section 2.4.

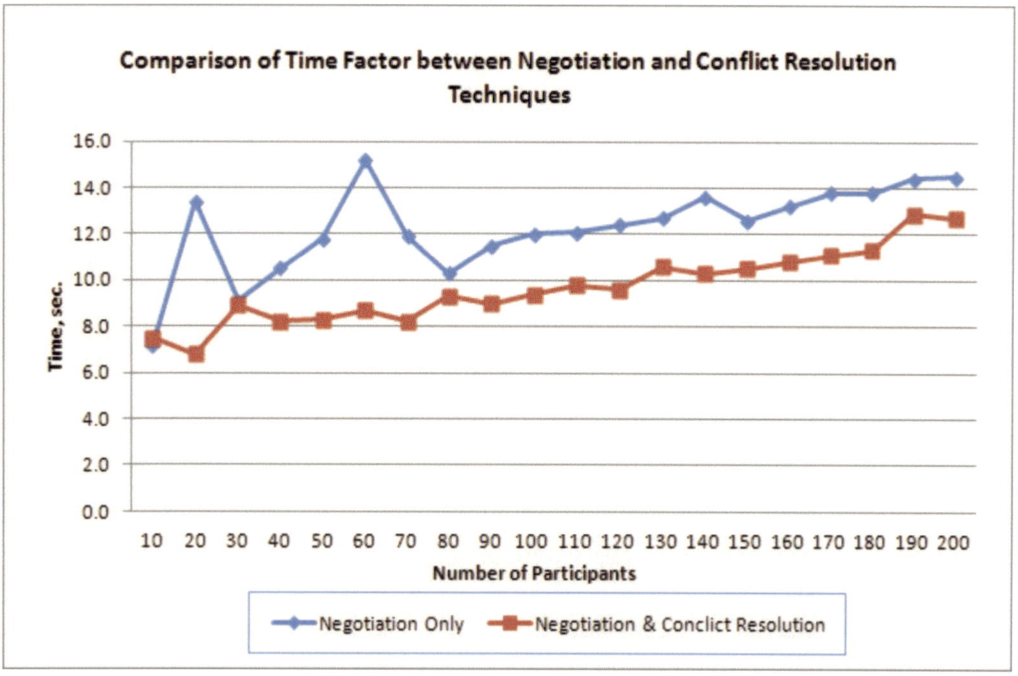

Fig. 6. The comparison of time factor in multi-agent negotiation between NO and CR.

5. Conclusion and future works

In this chapter, a conflict resolution model for multi-agent negotiation during grid resource federation is proposed and examined. Experimental results are shown that the conflict resolution method outperforms conventional negotiation method especially when VO has fewer participants. Besides, several automated agent negotiation approaches are compared and discussed in this review. A conflict resolution method, namely creative negotiation is successfully integrated into the SMNE protocol. Furthermore, several possible challenges for the implementation of SMNE protocol with intelligent agent are listed for further discussion.

Automation of several agent configurations such as negotiation strategies and tactics alteration in different situations, optimal parameters and threshold values assignment, are still opened issues for further improvement. Deployment of the proposed SMNE protocol into the real grid environment with several uncertainties such as network latency, system breakdown and hardware failure are yet to be analyzed. These issues remained as future work.

6. References

Alfieri R.; Cecchini R.; Ciaschini V.; Dell'Agnello L.; Frohner A.; Lorentey K. & Spataro F. (2005). From gridmap-file to VOMS: managing authorization in a Grid environment, *International Journal on Future Generation Computer Systems*, Vol.21, No.4, pp. 549-558, ISSN 0167-739X

Andreoli J.M. & Castellani, S. (2001). Towards a flexible middleware negotiation facility for distributed components, *Proceedings of DEXA "E-Negotiations" workshop*, pp. 732 - 736, ISBN 0-7695-1230-5, Munich, Germany, September, 2001

Andrieux A.; Czajkowski K.; Dan A.; Keahey K., Ludwig H.; Nakata T.; Pruyne J.; Rofrano J.; Tuecke S. & Xu M. (2005). *Web services agreement specification (WS-agreement)*, Version 2005/09, Global Grid Forum GRAAP-WG, http://xml.coverpages.org/WS-Agreement-13652.pdf

Barbuceanu M. & Lo W.K. (2000). A multi-attribute utility theoretic negotiation architecture for electronic commerce, *Proceedings of the 4th international conference on autonomous agents*, pp. 239-246, ISBN 1-581-13230-1, Barcelona, Spain, June, 2000

Bayucan A.; Henderson R.; Lesiak C.; Mann B.; Proett T. & Tweten D. (1999). *Portable Batch System: External reference specification*, NASA Ames Research Center, http://www.mcs.anl.gov/research/projects/openpbs/docs/v2_2_ers.pdf

Billikopf. G. E. (2003). Chapter 18: Creative Negotiation. In: *Labor Management Agriculture: Cultivating Personnel Productivity*, (2nd Ed.), 217-234, University of California, Agricultural and Natural Resources, Agricultural Issues Center, ISBN 1-885976-06-2, USA

Binmore K. & Vulkan N. (1999). Applying Game Theory to Automated Negotiation, *Journal of Netnomics*, Vol.1, No.1, pp. 1-9, ISSN 1385-9587

Braubach L.; Pokahr A. & Walczak A. (2006). *Jadex Tutorial*, Release 0.941, Distributed Systems Group, University of Hamburg http://jadex-agents.informatik.uni-hamburg.de/xwiki/bin/view/About/Overview

Chavez A.; Dreilinger D.; Guttman R. & Maes P. (1997). A Real-Life Experiment in Creating an Agent Marketplace, *Proceedings of the 2nd International Conference on Practical Application of Intelligent Agents and Multi-Agent Technology*, pp. 159-178, ISBN 0-9525-5546-8, Westminster Central Hall, London, UK, April, 1997

Cheng, W.K.; Chan, H.Y. & Fazilah, H. (2005). A Framework for Multi-Agent Negotiation System Using Adaptive Fuzzy Logic in Resource Allocation, *International Journal on Information Technology*, Vol.11, No.4, pp. 35-49, ISSN 0218-7957

Cheng, W.K.; Chan, H.Y. & Fazilah, H. (2006). Multi-Agent Negotiation System Using Adaptive Fuzzy Logic in Resource Allocation, *Proceedings of the Second IEEE International Conference on Distributed Framework of Multimedia Application*, pp. 7-13, ISBN 1-4244-0409-6, Penang, Malaysia, May, 2006

Cheng, W.K.; Ooi, B.Y. & Chan, H.Y. (2010). Resource Federation in Grid Using Automated Intelligent Agent Negotiation, *International Journal on Future Generation Computer Systems*, Vol.26, No.8, pp. 1116-1126, ISSN 0167-739X

Cray Inc. (1997). *Introducing NQE*, Technical Report IN-2153 2/97, Cray Inc., Seattle, Washington, USA

Czajkowski K.; Foster I.; Karonis N.; Kesselman C.; Martin S.; Smith W. & Tuecke S. (1998). A Resource Management Architecture for Metacomputing Systems, *4th Workshop on Job Scheduling Strategies for Parallel Processing*, pp. 62-82, ISBN 3-540-64825-9, Florida, March, 1998

Czajkowski K.; Ferguson D.F.; Foster I.; Frey J.; Graham S.; Sedukhin I.; Snelling D.; Tuecke S. & Vambenepe W. (2004). *The WS-Resource Framework*, Version 1.0, Globus Alliance and IBM, http://www.globus.org/wsrf/specs/ws-wsrf.pdf

Dave B. (2004). *RDF/XML Syntax Specification (Revised)*, World Wide Web Consortium (W3C), http://www.w3.org/TR/REC-rdf-syntax/

Djordjevic I. & Dimitrakos T. (2004). Towards dynamic security perimeters for virtual collaborative networks, *2nd International Conference on Trust Management*, pp. 191-205, ISBN 3-540-21312-0, Oxford, UK, March, 2004

FIPA. (2002). *FIPA ACL Message Structure Specification*, SC00061G, Foundation for Intelligent Physical Agents (FIPA), http://www.fipa.org/specs/fipa00061/index.html

Foster, I. & Kesselman, C. (1999). *The Grid: Blueprint for a New Computing Infrastructure*, Morgan Kaufmann, ISBN 1-55860-475-8, San Francisco, USA

Foster, I.; Kesselman, C. & Tuecke, S. (2001). The Anatomy of the Grid: Enabling Scalable Virtual Organization, *International Journal of Supercomputer Applications*, Vol.15. No.3, pp. 200-222, ISSN 1094-3420

Foster I.; Kesselman C.; Nick J.M. & Tuecke S. (2002). Grid Services for Distributed Systems Integration, *IEEE Computer*, Vol.35, No.6, pp. 37-46, ISSN 0018-9162

Foster, I.; Jennings, N.R. & Kesselman, C. (2004). Brain meets brawn: why Grid and agents need each other, *3rd International Conference on Autonomous Agents and Multi-Agent Systems*, pp. 8-15, ISBN 1-58113-864-4

Grimsaw A.S. & Wulf W.A. (1996). Legiona view from 50,000 Feet, *Proceedings of the 5th IEEE International Symposium on High Performance Distributed Computing*, pp. 89-99, ISBN 0-8186-7582-9, Syracuse, New York, USA, August, 1996

Kraus S. (2006). Automated Negotiation and Decision Making in Multiagent Environments, Multi-Agent-Systems and Applications, Vol.2086, pp. 150-172, ISBN 978-3-540-42312-6, Springer Berlin, 2006

Litzkow M.; Livny M. & Mutka M. (1998). Condor - A Hunter of Idle Workstations, *Proceedings of the 8th International Conference of Distributed Computing Systems*, pp. 104-111, ISBN 0-8186-0865-X, San Jose, CA , USA, June, 1998

Mailler R. & Lesser V. (2004). A Cooperative Mediation-based Protocol for Dynamic, Distributed Resource Allocation, *IEEE Transaction on Systems, Man, and Cybernetics, Part C: Applications and Reviews*, Vol.36, No.1, pp. 80-91, ISSN 1094-6977

Mobach D.G.A.; Overeinder B.J. & Brazier F.M.T. (2005). A Two-tiered Model of Negotiation based on Web Service Agreements, *Proceedings of the 3rd European Workshop on Multi-Agent Systems*, pp. 202-213, Brussels, Belgium, December, 2005

Moses T. (2005). *eXtensible Access Control Markup Language (XACML)*, Version 2.0, OASIS, http://docs.oasis-open.org/xacml/2.0/access_control-xacml-2.0-core-spec-os.pdf

Naqvi S. & Mori P. (2009). Security and trust management for virtual organisations: gridtrust approach, *IFIP International Conference on Trust Management 2009*, pp. 306-309, ISBN 978-3-642-02055-1, West Lafayette, Indiana, USA, June, 2009

Patrick H.C.K.; Li H.F. & Jeng J.J. (2004). WS-Negotiation - An Overview of Research Issues, *Proceedings of the 37th Annual Hawaii International Conference on System Sciences*, pp. 1-10, ISBN 0-7695-2056-1, Big Island, Hawaii, USA, January, 2004

Paurobally S.; Tamma V. & Wooldridge M. (2005). *Cooperation and Agreement between SemanticWeb Services*, World Wide Web Consortium (W3C), http://www.w3.org/2005/04/FSWS/Submissions/54/Paurobally sws2005.pdf

Rahwan I.; Sarvapali D.R.; Jennings N.R.; McBurney P.; Parsons S. & Sonenberg L. (2004). Argumentation-Based Negotiation, *The Knowledge Engineering Review*, Vol.18, No.4, pp. 343-375, ISSN 0269-8889

Raman R.; Livny M. & Solomon M. (1998). Matchmaking: distributed resource management for high throughput computing, 7th IEEE Int. Symp. High Performance Distributed Computing, pp. 140-146, ISBN 0-8186-8579-4, Chicago, Illinois, USA, July, 1998

Raman R.; Livny M. & Solomon M. (2003). Policy driven heterogeneous resource co-allocation with gangmatching, pp. 80-89, ISBN 0-7695-1965-2, Seattle, Washington, USA, June, 2003

Rao A. & Georgeff M. (1995). BDI Agents: from theory to practice, *Proceedings of the 1st International Conference on Multi-Agent Systems*, pp.312-319, ISBN 0-262-62102-9, San Francisco, California, USA, June, 1995

Roy J.L.; David M.S. & Barry B. (2009). Negotiation, 6th Edition, McGraw-Hill, ISBN 0-0729-7307-2, New York, USA

Russell, D.; Dew, P. & Djemame, K. (2004). Access Control for Dynamic Virtual Organisations, *Proceedings of the UK e-Science All Hands Meeting*, pp.332-339, ISBN 1-904425-21-6, Nottingham, UK, September, 2004

Sadri F.; Toni F. & Torroni P. (2002). Abductive logic programming architecture for negotiating agents, *Proceedings of the 8th European Conference on Logics in Artificial Intelligence*, Vol.2424, pp. 419-431, ISBN 3-540-44190-5, Cosenza, Italy, September, 2002

Sathi A. & Fox MS. (1990). *Constraint-directed Negotiation of Resource Reallocations*, Morgan Kaufmann, ISBN 0-273-08810-6, San Francisco, CA, USA

Smith R.G. (1980). The Contract Net Protocol: High-Level Communication and Control in a Distributed Problem Solver, *IEEE Transactions on Computers*, Vol.29, No.12, pp. 1104-1113, ISSN 0018-9340

Ströbel, M. & Weinhardt, C. (2003). The Montreal Taxonomy for Electronic Negotiation, *Journal Group Decision and Negotiation*, Vol.12, pp. 143-164, ISSN 1572-9907

Sycara K. (1989). Multi-agent compromise via negotiation, *Distributed Artificial Intelligence*, Vol.2, pp. 119-139, ISBN 0-273-08810-6, Morgan Kaufmann, San Mateo, California, USA, 1989

Tsang, E.P.K. (1993). *Foundations of Constraint Satisfaction*, Academic Press Limited, ISBN 0-12-701610-4, London and San Diego, UK

Waeldrich O.; Battré D.; Brazier F.; Clark K.; Oey M.; Papaspyrou A.; Wieder P. & Ziegler W. (2011). *WS-Agreement Negotiation*, Version 1.0, Open Grid Forum, http://www.gridforum.org/documents/GFD.193.pdf

Venugopal S.; Chu X. & Buyya R. (2008). A negotiation mechanism for advance resource reservations using the alternate offers protocol, *16th International Workshop on Quality of Service*, pp. 40-49, ISBN 978-1-4244-2084-1, Netherlands, June, 2008

Xie, J.M. & Qi, D.Y. (2006). A Spaces Based Coordination Model for Virtual Organizations, *International Symposium on Applications and the Internet*, pp. 23-27, ISBN 0-7695-2508-3, Phoenix, Arizona, USA, January, 2006

Zhou S.; Zheng X.; Wang J. & Delisle P. (1993). Utopia: a Load Sharing Facility for Large, Heterogeneous Distributed Computer Systems, *International Journal on Software: Practice and Experience*, Vol.23, No.12, pp. 1305-13, ISSN 1097-024X

3

Homogeneous and Heterogeneous Agents in Electronic Auctions

Jacob Sow, Patricia Anthony and Chong Mun Ho
Universiti Malaysia Sabah
Malaysia

1. Introduction

When considering the agents mediated electronic marketplace, agents play an active role in both sellers and buyers sides. A seller agent may advertise its products in the market, placing the selling price and looking for the potential buyers in the market. On the other hand, a buyer agent would look for the desired goods or services requested by its user and it has a task to bargain about the price of the products and find the best deal (Dignum, 2001). Besides that, due to the rapid growth of Information Technology and popularities of the Internet, more trading that could be done in bricks and mortar is now available without geographical constraint by using the computer and the Internet. Therefore, sellers are now looking for a larger group of potential buyers while buyers are looking for a better offer of their desired goods in the online marketplace.

1.1 Online auctions

An auction is a bidding mechanism, described by a set of auction rules that specifies how the winner is determined and how much to be paid (Wolfstetter, 1999). By auctioning, sellers find a way to determine the actual values of the items being auctioned especially those items which are hard in valuation process. By auctioning also, items are allocated to the bidders who have the highest valuation. Therefore, auction mechanism is an interesting topic to be studied since it provides an approach to the price formation of the item. Besides, McAfee and McMillan (1987) argued that studying auction is closer to applications than other mathematical economics. The auction theory explains the existence of certain trading institutions and may suggest improvements in these institutions.

In the virtual marketplace which sells a single object, there are basically four types of online auction protocols, namely the ascending-price (English) auction, the descending-price (Dutch) auction, the first-price sealed bid auction and the second-price sealed bid (Vickrey) auction. In the ascending-price (English) auction, sellers start at a low price and the price is successively raised by bidders until the auction end time is reached. The bidder with the highest bid wins the auction and pays based on the bid submitted.

The descending-price (Dutch) auction is the opposite of an English auction. An auctioneer starts announcing an auction with an initial high price. This high price is normally higher than the item's actual price. The initial bid will be lowered progressively until there is an offer from a bidder to claim the item. The winner pays the price offered.

The first-price sealed bid auction and the second-price sealed bid auction are quite similar in terms of the bid submission. Interested bidders submit their bids privately and these bids are concealed until the auction ends. When the auction ends, those concealed bids are disclosed. Bidder with the highest bid will be identified as the winner. However, in the former auction type, the winner pays for the item with his bid, but the second highest bid in the latter type of auction is paid.

Regardless of which auction protocols are used in the online auctions, there are many online auction sites that are available on the Internet. Moreover, as this mechanism is accepted by more people, the number of auctions conducted in this virtual marketplace is increasing drastically. Thus, a bidder would find it very hard to find a suitable auction to participate. This problem leads to a question, is there any alternative method to overcome this dilemma? The answer can be found by using agent technology.

1.2 Agent technology

According to Jennings and Wooldridge (1998), an intelligent agent is a computer entity that is capable of flexible autonomous action in order to meet its design objectives. The term flexible here means that an intelligent agent should be responsive, proactive and social. These intelligent agents should solve their problems encountered in their environment without direct intervention of human or other agents. Furthermore, as intelligent agents, they have their own goals to be achieved (Dignum, 2001). So, when the outside world is changed, they should not simply react to these changes; they should also exhibit opportunistic, goal-directed behaviors and take initiatives where appropriate to achieve their primary objective. On the other hand, they should perceive their environment and respond consistently to changes that occur. This property somehow neutralizes the pro-activeness of agents. It prevents agents from trying to achieve their goals without considering the achievability of the goals. They must also interact with one another (other agents or human) in order to complete their goals and help others with their problems.

To this end, an agent system may seem to be similar to an object-oriented system. For example, an object in the object–oriented system encapsulates some states and has control over these states. These states can only be accessed or modified via the methods provided by the object. So does the agent. But the behaviors of an agent are also encapsulated. For example, if there is an object X that invokes a method m on object Y, then Y has no control over whether m is executed or not. In this sense, Y is not autonomous since it has no control over its own actions. On the other hand, agent has control over its behaviors or actions. The interaction among the agents is more in the request and response manner. An agent may request an action to be done by another agent. But the decision on whether the action is performed lies solely with the recipient agent.

Besides that, intelligent agents in online auctions never overbid. According to Lee and Malmendier (2007), human bidders often overbid their private valuations on items desired. Thus, by using intelligent agents, human bidders can be rest assured that overbidding does not occur to them since agents never bid above the maximum values provided by them.

Due to the agent's properties and capabilities, agent technology is acceptable in electronic commerce, particularly in the online auction. By applying agent technology in online auction, the challenges stated in Section 1.1 may be greatly lightened. However, knowing which auction to bid is not sufficient to guarantee that the agents can win the auction. It also needs to consider how much should a bidder submit and its efficiency when competing with other human bidders or other bidder agents.

1.3 Bidding issues

When agents are deployed in online auction marketplaces, their owners usually explicitly inform them the maximum price of an item. Nonetheless, winning an auction with a lower bid indicates that the agent not only complete its task of obtaining the item, but also increases the profit or utility of the winner and vice-versa. Hence, many researchers have been studying different bidding strategies in different auction protocols with the hope to maximize the winner's satisfaction. Some of these strategies are reviewed and developed from the perspective of game theory (Yang & Lu, 2007), neuro-fuzzy approach (He *et al.*, 2004, 2006; Lin *et al.*, 2006), grey theory predictive models (Lim *et al.*, 2007; 2008), heuristic models (Anthony & Jennings, 2003; Yuen *et al.*, 2006) or as from bidders' behaviors (Roth & Ockenfels, 2002).

Due to different available bidding strategies and studies on auction environment, more experienced or advanced bidders may obtain useful information to strategize their bidding behaviors in order to increase their winning probabilities. It is even more complicated when agent technology is implemented into this environment. On the one hand, with the help of intelligent agents, bidders can ease their searching and monitoring or even bidding tasks to them and be regularly informed. On the other hand, due to the capability of computational advantages, bidder agents may have more freedom to select and participate in different auctions to purchase their desired goods. In other words, sellers are now facing greater competition from around the world to attract buyers while human bidders are oppressed and have to make decision very carefully to outbid their counterparts.

From another perspective, when homogeneous intelligent agents and heterogeneous intelligent agents are implemented in the marketplace, sellers may react differently due to the market economy and their revenues generated. A seller may assume that as more bidder agents are found in their auctions, this would lower their auction closing prices. It is because agents never overbid and they make wider survey than human bidders before participating in any auctions on the Internet. Nonetheless, as agent technology is becoming a dominant trend in developing online auctions mechanism, it would be interesting to study the reaction of sellers when they are confronted with bidder agents of single type and multiple types.

Hence, this chapter attempts to study the impacts resulted from utilizing intelligent agents in the online auction marketplace. More specifically, the competitions among standard bidders and intelligent agents with various bidding strategies are to be analyzed. Standard bidders are to be categorized into 3 types according to their respective risk attitudes while intelligent agents are to be equipped with a heuristic bidding strategy, the greedy bidding strategy and the sniping strategy. From these competitions, the performance of each type of bidders and agents are to be examined. Furthermore, sellers' reaction on the implementation of bidder agents is briefly examined. A simulated marketplace will be used to conduct these experiments and for further analysis.

The rest of the chapter is arranged as follow: Section 2 discusses the related works on online English auctions, bidding strategies and bidder agents developed by other researchers. In the next section, the architecture of the simulated marketplace is described. In Section 4, performances of different bidders are analyzed. Lastly, this paper ends with conclusions and suggestions for future works.

2. Literature review

2.1 Online english auctions

In English auction, a price is successively raised through submitting new bids by bidders until there is only one bidder who is willing to buy the item being auctioned (McAfee & McMillan, 1987). In this type of auction, all bids submitted are made known to every participant immediately. Therefore, interested bidders can submit their bids to outbid the current highest bidder. Besides that, before an auction is started, the seller may set a hidden price which indicates the minimum price he is willing to sell the item. This hidden price is commonly known as the seller's reserve price. By implementing this reserve price, the item will only be sold if the closing price of an auction is not less than that. More interestingly, sometimes, the English auction is also known as the second highest price auction since the winner only pays a price that is equivalent to the second highest bidder's valuation.

Many researchers have shown their interests in the field of auction, especially on the English auction protocol since it is the most commonly accepted and widely implemented protocol in selling a single object. Hu and Bolivar (2008) showed their interest in online auctions efficiency, particularly on eBay auctions. They investigated and analyzed multiple online auction properties including consumer surplus and their cross-relationships. In their data analysis, they implemented consumer surplus ratio (CSR) as a measurement to evaluate the winners' profit over the final value. Also, they utilized the concept of median instead of average in this CSR in order to reduce the influence of sparse outliers. By comparing the consumer surplus ratio, they found that the surplus ratio is generally impacted by the nature of the market and the ability to find a replacement. Rareness itself makes the valuation process difficult and thus is leading to high surplus ratios.

Besides that, overbidding is one of the interesting scenarios found in online auctions. Overbidding is a phenomenon in which the winner of an auction finds himself paying too much to purchase the item being auctioned after the auction closes. Lee and Malmendier (2007) studied this phenomenon and found that such overbidding affects both private-value and common-value settings. In the work conducted, they found that even experienced bidders fell into this bidder's curse. At first they may remember the upper limit of the bids. However, this memory fades out as time goes by. Besides that, the cost of switching from auctions to auctions or to fixed price transaction, the structure of outbid messages and the extra winning utility were introduced to explain the bidder's curse. From another perspective, they suggested that sellers may benefit from such scenario in terms of their revenue earned.

David *et al.* (2005) conducted their research in optimal design of English auctions with discrete bid levels. In their research, they aimed to provide the revenue maximizing design for this type of English auction. They identified that there is a case which two or more bidders are found in the same bid level and none of them can further increase the current price to another higher level. Thus, one of them is randomly selected as the current highest bidder and eventually the winner of the auction. Seller's revenue in this case was underestimated since the second highest bid may not be the second highest bidder's valuation and the outcome may not be efficient as the item is not necessarily purchased by the bidder with the highest valuation. In order to maximize the revenue obtained in this case, they proposed and examined by empirical experiments that as the number of bidders increases, the bid levels become increasingly closer spaced. In their experiments, they also found that the optimal reserve price increases as more bidders participate in the auction.

2.2 Bidder's common behaviors

There are commonly three distinct types of risk behaviors considered, namely risk aversion (RA), risk neutral (RN) and risk seeking (RS). Generally, a RA bidder is willing to compromise his profit to reduce the risk or uncertainty (the loss in an auction). With the same perspective, a RS bidder is willing to take the risk without giving up his profit. Lastly, a bidder is considered as RN if he is not affected by either the risks that come from the uncertainty he faces or the maximized profit (Watson, 2004). Of course, in different situations, the risk considered is varied according to the focus of the study. Also, the degree of risk-aversion or risk seeking are greatly dependent on how much from a bidder's profit he is willing to sacrifice or how risky it is if he loses in an auction respectively. There are many researchers studying the impact contributed by these risks in different auctions such as McAfee and McMillan (1987), Klemperer (1999), Wolfstetter (1999) and Talluri and Ryzin (2004).

On the other hand, Ockenfels and Roth mentioned in their respective papers (Ockenfels & Roth, 2002, 2006; Roth & Ockenfels, 2002) that many bidders (or their agents) tend to submit their bids late (this is also referred to as bid sniping). Hu and Bolivar (2008) also supported this finding by using eBay data collected. According to them, sniping is defined as the process of watching a timed online auction, placing a winning bid at the very last possible moment before an auction is ended. Sniping has an advantage of giving no time to other bidders to respond when they are outbid. Furthermore, they found that by performing sniping strategy, bidding wars are avoided among bidders and thus it will increase the expected bidder profits while decreasing the seller revenues. Therefore, the last-minute bidding is not simply due to naïve time-dependent bidding, but it responds to the strategic structure of the auction format in a predictable way.

As the online auction is widely implemented and practiced in the trading community, there are hundreds of thousands of different auctions running simultaneously. Thus, soon bidders will find that choosing an auction is not an easy task. It is even more troublesome if several desired auctions come from different auction houses. Consequently, searching and monitoring those auctions become time consuming tasks. Fortunately, due to the proliferation of agent technology, these problems may be solved or greatly reduced by implementing this technology into the online auctions.

2.3 Intelligent agents in online english auctions

As mentioned by Dignum (2001), agents will only be used as user representatives if the benefits of using an agent are high and the trust that an agent will realize them is high. Due to the furtherance of the artificial intelligence and computer technology, using such technology in online auctions is at minimal cost.

First of all, Anthony and Jennings (2003) developed a bidding agent equipped with a heuristic bidding strategy for multiple heterogeneous auctions. This bidding strategy consists of four tactics, namely the remaining time tactic, the remaining auctions tactic, the desire for bargain tactic and the desperateness tactic. By combining these tactics and taking into account the priority of these tactics, a suggested bid is generated to its bidder and is to be used in the auction desired.

Besides that, Yuen *et al.* (2006) investigated utility maximizing bidding heuristics for agents that participate in multiple heterogeneous auctions in which auction format and their start and end times might be varied. In their proposed bidding strategy, all four heuristic strategies outperformed the two benchmark strategies (greedy strategy and random strategy) used in their experiment.

In other studies conducted by Lim *et al.* (2007, 2008), they argued that an intelligent agent would greatly help its bidder if the closing price of an auction is predicted successfully. Therefore, they studied several prediction models (ARIMA model, artificial neural network with backpropagation model and the grey theory prediction model) and found out that the grey prediction model successfully forecasted the most accurate data among these three prediction models. Furthermore, the concept of moving data was implemented to increase the accuracy of the predicted price.

He *et al.* (2004, 2006) focused their interest on agent's bidding strategy that is incorporated with neuro-fuzzy techniques, the Earliest Closest First heuristic algorithm. It identifies auctions that are most suited to the bidders' requirements and according to their risk attitudes, bids in some other auctions that have approximately similar expected return, but which close earlier than those in the best return set. The greedy strategy, the fixed auction strategy and the average strategy were used to make comparison with their proposed strategy. From the results obtained, the Earliest Closest First algorithm performed better among these strategies considered.

Park *et al.* (1999) developed an adaptive bidding strategy that would be used by sellers in continuous double auction and it is implemented based on stochastic modeling. They argued that this strategy is capable of taking the dynamics and uncertainties of the auctions into account and therefore agents equipped with this strategy receive higher profit in the auctions participated. However, due to the computational cost and time consumption in this strategy, they further modified the strategy such that an agent equipped with this strategy might decide the time of using it.

Ford *et al.* (2010) concentrated their research on layered bidding strategies for autonomous bidding agents. In their proposed strategies, a complex strategy (top layer) is formed from complex strategies or simple strategies (middle layer); while a simple strategy consists of atomic bidding actions (bottom layer). Users can easily specify a user defined strategy by manipulating the layers. Besides that, they proposed 2 algorithms that would convert those strategies into rule-based bidding strategies which will be executed by the bidding agents and for agents' reasoning purposes.

From the researches and studies discussed and reviewed in this section, it can be seen that studying online auction is not a new topic. By equipping different bidding strategies, computer agents are integrated to make decision in auctions marketplace on their users' behalf. However, there are still other areas in online auctions where researchers may explore. One of them is the market economy when a market is fully populated by homogeneous agents and heterogeneous agents. Besides that, as the implementation of agent technology becomes more acceptable in the online auction marketplace, sellers' reactions when confronting with them may be an interesting subject to be studied.

3. Simulated online auction marketplace

There are many successful online auction houses that are running on the Internet such as eBay. However, due to different perspectives of houses administrators and researchers, data retrieval from these auction houses is restrictive if not impossible. Furthermore, certain information may not be extracted easily due to the legal responsibilities and sometimes data extraction is subject to disclosure of companies' privacy. Therefore, simulated online auction marketplace becomes an alternative testing platform for researchers to conduct their experiments and retrieve data for further analyses.

In this work, a simulated online auction marketplace is used to simulate a real auction house where multiple English auctions are conducted. Since they may have different start and end times, they are run concurrently in the auction house. Besides that, all auctions in this marketplace are the symmetric independent private values (SIPV) auctions (Matthews, 1995; Wolfstetter, 1999).

In the setting phase, researchers can set a number of auctions to be conducted in this simulation in a range of 1 to 100 inclusive. While the number of auctions is determined by researchers, each auction's start and end times are randomly assigned by the system. By doing so, these simulated concurrent English auctions are similar to the one found in the real online auction houses. Secondly, there are two types of bidders, a group of standard bidders and a group of bidders who use agent technology. Researchers can manually assign the number of standard bidders found in the marketplace in a range of 0 to 3000 inclusive and their risk behaviors. Next, the number of intelligent agents can be assigned in a range of 0 to 3000 inclusive with three different bidding strategies, namely the greedy strategy (Byde, 2002), the sniping strategy (Ockenfels & Roth, 2002, 2006; Roth & Ockenfels, 2002; Hu & Bolivar, 2008) and a heuristic bidding strategy (Anthony & Jennings, 2003). The greedy strategy is selected because of its bidding attribute. Some bidders may use their agents to look for auctions with the lowest current bids. By doing so, they wish to purchase the items with minimal prices. Next, agents that are equipped with the heuristic bidding strategy selected here would represent another group of bidders who are well prepared before participating in any auction. They do not only consider the current bid, but also the number of similar auctions available, the timeline of obtaining the items if won and how desperate they are in procuring the items. Lastly, the sniping strategy is taken into account because it avoids bidding war (Ockenfels & Roth, 2002, 2006; Roth & Ockenfels, 2002). Moreover, another group of bidders who are impatient with longer auction closing time and keen to obtain the items desired without wasting time on surveying other auctions may prefer this strategy.

Next, the system prepares the marketplace by generating auctions, sellers, both standard bidders and intelligent agents according to the predefined settings. Each auction is assigned a reserve price of the item randomly based on a normal distribution. This normal distribution is generated by providing a mean value and a standard deviation value of the actual closing prices collected from Internet auctions. By doing so, the marketplace simulates the real online auctions pricing scenario. Besides that, the standard bidders and the intelligent agents are assigned their private valuations from the same normal distribution used for the item's reserve price generation. These values are taken as the maximum values that they are willing to pay in obtaining the goods. After that, standard bidders are assigned to different auctions by the system. Whenever it is possible, standard bidders are distributed evenly to all the auctions generated. They are treated as the faithful bidders as they do not move from an auction to another. On the other hand, intelligent agents situate in the marketplace. Every time there is a bidding process conducted, these intelligent agents would find the most promising auction to participate.

Lastly, auctions are started automatically if their start time is reached. Both standard bidders and intelligent agents are free to submit their bids according to their criteria and preferences. In this marketplace, a universal time is used and every time step is discrete and indivisible. In each time step, all auctions are checked if they are active. For each active auction, a standard bidder will be chosen randomly to submit a bid. At the same time, if there is any intelligent agent interested in submitting its bid in the same auction, a competition among the selected standard bidder and the intelligent agent(s) occurs. As a result, a higher bid would outbid lower bids. Besides that, if an auction's end time is reached, the seller would announce the bidder with the highest bid as the winner of that auction if the auctions are closed with trading. Throughout the whole bidding process of different auctions conducted, their bidding histories are recorded for data analyses.

3.1 Participants in the simulated online auction marketplace

In this simulated platform, sellers are the owners of the item to be auctioned and are also the auctioneers who conduct the auctions. They wish to sell their products through English auction protocol. Besides that, there are bidders in these auctions with the aim to obtain the desired goods. They are categorized further into two groups according to the usage of agent technology, the standard bidders and the bidders who utilize intelligent agents.

3.1.1 Standard bidders and bidding behaviors

Standard bidders do not implement any agents to act on their behalf. They would personally join an auction and submit a bid whenever it is possible. Furthermore, these standard bidders can also be categorized as faithful bidders since they will stay in an auction until they win that auction or when their private valuation is exceeded. Moreover, as long as the current bid in an auction is lower than their private valuations, they would submit their bids in the auction. However, bid increments vary depending on the bidders' risk behaviors.

There are 3 types of risk attitudes considered in this simulated marketplace, namely the risk aversion (RA), risk neutral (RN) and risk seeking (RS). In this marketplace, bidders face the risk of not winning an auction at the lowest closing price. By understanding the risk mentioned here, a RA bidder is afraid that he may pay an unnecessary higher price conditional on winning the auction. On the other hand, a RN bidder has no difference between paying more or less conditional on winning an auction. Lastly, a RS bidder is not afraid of paying an unnecessary higher price conditional on winning an auction. A RA bidder would start bidding at a minimal bid increment (randomly chosen from a range of 1 to 3 inclusive). By doing so, he hopes to submit a bid that is as minimal as possible which in turn would win the auction. However, their bidding strategy changes towards the end of an auction. If they are not the current highest bidder, they would bid more aggressively (randomly chosen from a range of 7 to 9 inclusive) to increase the probability of becoming the current highest bidder and eventually win the auction.

On the other hand, a RS bidder would bid aggressively from the beginning of an auction (drawn randomly from a range of 7 to 9 inclusive). They are less concerned on paying too much as long as he obtains the item desired within his valuation. Moreover, they try to frighten other bidders by bidding aggressively. Nonetheless, as the time goes by, a RS bidder who is not the current highest bidder would try his best to become the leading bidder in the auction. But his private valuation is approaching due to his aggressive bidding from the beginning of an auction. Therefore, by realizing this fact, he changes his bidding strategy from an aggressive act to a more conservative way. He reduces his bid increment choices (in a range of 1 to 3 inclusive) to avoid bidding over his private valuation.

At the same time, a RN bidder starts his bidding with a different strategy. Since he is indifferent with the risk of paying unnecessary higher price with the hope of winning an auction, he would bid constantly in his bid increment. In other words, he would not change his bid increment in his bidding process. His bid increment is almost a constant value from the beginning of an auction until the auction is closed (randomly drawn from a range of 4 to 6 inclusive).

Regardless of the risk attitudes, the bid increments used in this simulated auction house are arbitrary values. They are distributed uniformly and thus have equal chances to be selected. Any other value can be used to simulate their bidding behaviors. Besides that, these scenarios may be further explained by using the von Neumann-Morgenstern utility as explained by Bierman (1998).

When explaining a bidder's strategy with von Neumann-Morgenstern utility, the marginal utility and the motivation of submitting high or low bid are correlated. According to Fig. 1, when a RA bidder submits the first bid, if he wins at this point, he gains the maximum profit as indicated by the end point at the right most. Nevertheless, normally an auction receives more bids from other bidders. Therefore, he would continue to submit more bids until he is the leading bidder in the auction. So, the obtained profit is shifted to the left as more bids are submitted. As the profit decreases from right to left of the graph, the marginal utilities of different bids are compared. As indicated in the figure, the marginal utility from the first bid to second bid submitted is relatively smaller than the marginal utility from the latter bids. This marginal utility becomes larger when more bids are submitted. Therefore, a RA bidder would be motivated to submit a larger bid towards the end of an auction.

Next, when a RN bidder submits his first bid and if he wins, he obtains his maximum profit from the auction as indicated by the end point at the right most of the Fig. 2. However, as more bidders participate in the same auction, he starts to counter bid his competitors by submitting subsequent bids. Hence, the profit gained from winning the auction is shifted to the left of the graph as more bids submitted. Nevertheless, the marginal utilities of his bids are constantly observed. It can be explained as the motivation of submitting subsequent bids by a RN bidder is always the same. Consequently, a RN bidder would never change his bids either from the beginning of an auction or towards the end of the auction.

Lastly, in Fig. 3, the end point located at the right most of the graph indicates the maximum profit obtained by a RS bidder if he wins an auction with his first bid. Nonetheless, more bids are usually required before winning an auction. Thus, the profit is shifted to the left of the graph. When comparing the marginal utility of each bid submitted, those earlier bids have larger marginal utilities than those bids submitted later. Thus, a RS bidder tends to submit larger bid increments at the beginning of an auction rather than towards the end of the auction.

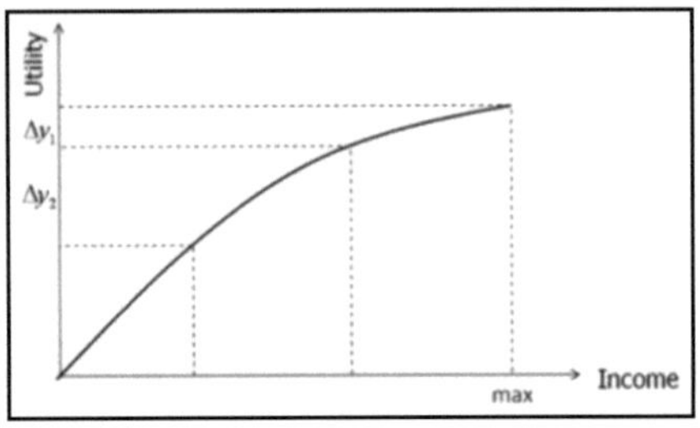

Fig. 1. Risk-averse Bidder's von Neumann-Morgenstern Utility.

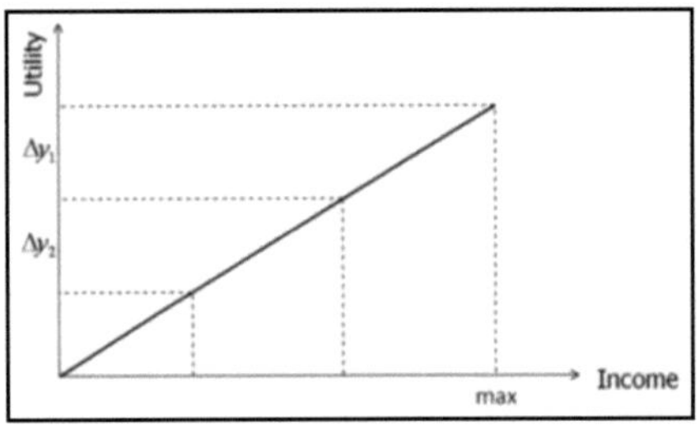

Fig. 2. Risk Neutral Bidder's von Neumann-Morgenstern Utility.

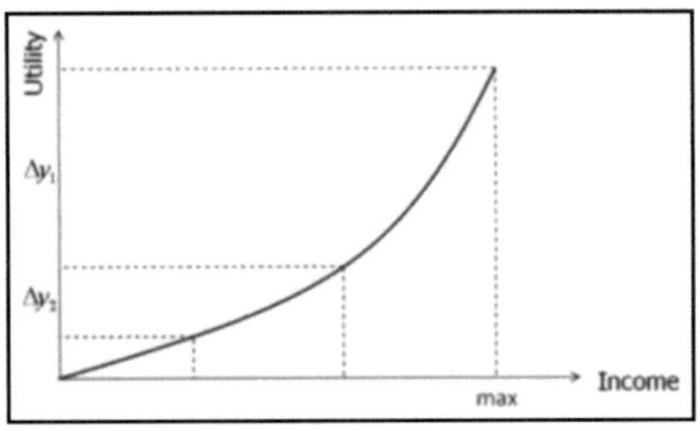

Fig. 3. Risk Seeking Bidder's von Neumann-Morgenstern Utility.

3.1.2 Intelligent agents and bidding behaviors

Another type of bidders utilizes intelligent agent technology to represent them in bidding process. Therefore, this type of bidders saves time on searching, monitoring and participating in an auction. These intelligent agents in this simulated marketplace are equipped with different bidding strategies according to the experimental setup. Firstly, by using greedy strategy, an agent would always look for an auction with the lowest current bid as its target auction. Then it would increase the current bid with an increment from a range of 1 to 10 randomly. These values in the range are just arbitrary values. In the case where multiple auctions are found to have the lowest current price, the first auction found is to be selected as the target auction for an agent (Fig. 4).

while ($t < t_{max}$) and (item not obtained = true)

    Build active auctions list

    List all auctions that are active before t_{max}.

    Select target auction as one that has the lowest current bid.

    Calculate the new bid, current bid + randomize bid increment.

    Bid in the target auction with the new bid.

End while

where t is the current universal time across all auctions, t_{max} is the agent's allocated bidding time by when it must obtain the goods or leave the auctions.

Fig. 4. The Top-level Algorithm for the Greedy Agent.

Secondly, those agents equipped with the sniping strategy would hold their bids until the last time step of an auction with the hope of outbidding others while give them insufficient time to react. Their sniped bids are a sum of the current bid of an auction with an increment from a range of 1 to 10 (Fig. 5). Again, these values are just arbitrary values. Similarly, when there is more than an auction closes on the last possible time step, the first auction found by an agent would be selected as its target auction.

while ($t < t_{max}$) *and* (item not obtained = *true*)

    Build active auctions list

    List all auctions that are active before t_{max}.

    Select target auction as one that has t = end time - 1.

    Calculate the new bid, current bid + randomize bid increment.

    Bid in the target auction with the new bid.

End while

where t is the current universal time across all auctions, t_{max} is the agent's allocated bidding time by when it must obtain the goods or leave the auctions.

Fig. 5. The Top-level Algorithm for the Sniping Agent.

Lastly, the Heuristic strategy consists of four tactics used in the bidding process, namely the remaining time tactic, the remaining auction tactic, the desire for bargaining and the desperateness of obtaining the item. In the first tactic, as every agent has its own time constraint, this tactic tackles with this limitation. Meanwhile, the second tactic handles the consideration of remaining auctions that are still available before an agent's time is reached. Thirdly, if an agent is willing to bargain the price of an item desired, it would bid minimally to avoid paying a high price to win an auction. Finally, if an agent is desperate in obtaining an item from an auction, it would submit higher bids to increase its probability of winning that auction. After receiving the new suggested bid from the strategy, this new suggested bid is further modified if necessary (Fig. 6).

Next, in order to decide which potential auctions to be participated, these Heuristic agents calculate the expected utility of each auction by using the equations below:

$$\text{expected utility} = P_i(v)U_i(v) \tag{1}$$

and

$$\mathrm{U_i}(v) = \frac{pr - v}{pr} \tag{2}$$

where $P_i(v)$ is the probability of winning an auction i at a bid v, $U_i(v)$ is the utility of an auction i at a bid v, pr is the agent's private valuation. After calculating the expected utilities of all auctions available, an auction with the highest expected utility is selected as the most promising auction. The agent would participate in the most promising auction with the bid received from its bidding strategy.

while ($t < t_{\max}$) *and* (item not obtained = *true*)

Build active auctions list

List all auctions that are active before $t_{\max}$.

Calculate the new suggested bid using the agent's strategy.

If the difference(suggested bid, current bid) > a preset threshold,

new suggested bid = current bid + a portion of difference

Select potential auctions from active auctions list to bid in.

Select target auction as one that maximizes agent's expected utility.

Bid in the target auction with the new suggested bid.

End while

where t is the current universal time across all auctions, $t_{\max}$ is the agent's allocated bidding time by when it must obtain the goods or leave the auctions.

Fig. 6. The Top-level Algorithm for the Heuristic Bidding Agent.

In the next section, different experiments are performed according to the different auction requirements. Under different settings, from auction to a more general view of the marketplace are to be analyzed especially from the economic perspective.

4. Experimental setup and results

In this section, several empirical experiments are designed and conducted. Firstly, heterogeneous standard bidders will compete with homogeneous intelligent agents in an auction market. Secondly, competition occurs among heterogeneous standard bidders and heterogeneous intelligent agents. Thirdly, markets that are populated by homogeneous intelligent agents and heterogeneous intelligent agents are studied and analyzed.

4.1 Methods of measurements

In these empirical experiments conducted, several methods are utilized to evaluate the performance of different bidders and agents. They are the average winner's utility, the average number of winning auctions, the average closing price and the consumer surplus ratio. These methods are measured according to the types of different participants.

4.1.1 Average winner's utility

In every auction traded successfully, winner obtains certain profit from winning the auction. Besides that, since different bidders and agents may have different private valuations generated from the same normal distribution, this profit is evaluated as a ratio with respect to their own private valuations. By doing so, the factor of their different private valuations which would lead to various gains is greatly eliminated. To calculate the average winner's utility, the following mathematical equations are used:

$$U_{ij}(v) = \frac{Pr_i - v_j}{Pr_i} + c \tag{3}$$

and

$$\bar{U}_i(v) = \frac{\sum_{j=1}^{n_i} U_{ij}(v)}{n_i} \tag{4}$$

where $U_{ij}(v)$ is the winner's utility of auction j gained by winners of type i, Pr_i is the private valuation of the winner of type i, v_j is the winning bid of auction j, c is an arbitrary constant set to 0.001, $\bar{U}_i(v)$ is the average winner's utility of type i, n_i is the number of auctions won by winners of type i. In Equation 3, a constant c is used to ensure that in the worst case where a winner pays his maximum valuation to purchase the item being auctioned, he still deserves a small gain compared to those who lose in the same auction.

4.1.2 Average number of winning auctions

In this method, auctions won by different groups of bidders and agents are counted into their respective categories. This method is concerned with the number of winning auctions in a society of a certain type of winners. To calculate the average number of winning auctions for a given bidder or agent in the marketplace, the following equation is used:

$$\overline{W_i} = \frac{\sum_1^n \text{number of auctions won by winners of type } i}{n} \quad (5)$$

where $\overline{W_i}$ is the average number of auctions won by winners of type i, n is the number of runs conducted in the experiment.

4.1.3 Average closing price

The third measurement is the average closing price. Based on this measurement, the performance of the winners is evaluated in terms of the price paid to purchase the item desired.

$$\bar{C_i} = \frac{\sum_{j=1}^{n_i} C_{ij}}{n_i} \quad (6)$$

where, C_{ij} is the winning bid of auction j submitted by winners of type i, n_i is the number of auctions won by winners of type i.

4.1.4 Average consumer surplus ratio

The consumer surplus ratio (CSR) is introduced by Hu and Bolivar (2008) which considers the number of bids found in an auction and the median number of bids across all the auctions conducted. This ratio is used to show the surplus gained by each winner with respect to his private valuation. Hence, it is similar to the average winner's utility. However, it considers also the number of bids received in each auction and the median number of bids received across all the auctions available. It is assumed that an auction with more bids submitted will most probably ends with higher price compared to auctions with less bids. In this research, intelligent agents are free to select the auction to participate based on their selection model. So, in a market where multiple agents of different types are found, the considerations in this ratio would reduce the extreme bids submitted and the influence of number of bids. This ratio is evaluated as follow:

$$CSR_j = \text{Median}_{\forall j}\left(\frac{\left(V_{H_i} - V_{F_i}\right)\cdot(N_i + N_m)}{V_{F_i}\cdot N_i + V_{H_i}\cdot N_m}\right) \quad (7)$$

and

$$\overline{\mathrm{CSR_j}} = \frac{\sum_1^n \mathrm{CSR_j}}{\mathrm{n}} \quad (8)$$

where j is the type of winners, $V_{H_i}$is the winner's private valuation in auction i, V_{F_i} is the final winning bid in auction i, N_i is the number of bids of item i, N_m is the median number of bids across all the auctions conducted, $\overline{CSR_j}$ is the average CSR of winners of type j, n is the number of runs conducted in the experiment. A high value in this CSR would indicate that the winner receives high surplus compared to his own private valuation after minimizing the influences as stated in the considerations.

4.1.5 Average seller's utility

On the other hand, as suggested by Krishna (2002), sellers extract more revenues from auctions with higher number of bidders. In this market, some auctions may receive more bids compared to other auctions. Therefore, by using the ratio instead of the surplus, the factor of having different values of winning bids in different auctions is minimized. The equation is given as below:

$$R_j(v) = \frac{v_j - RP_j}{v_j} \tag{9}$$

and

$$\bar{R}(v) = \frac{\sum_{j=1}^{n} R_j(v)}{n} \tag{10}$$

where $R_j(v)$ is the seller's utility of auction j, v_j is the winning bid of auction j, RP_j is the seller's reserved price of auction j, $\bar{R}(v)$ is the average seller's utility, n is the number of auctions that are closed with winner.

4.2 Normal distribution of data

Before any experiment is conducted, data generated from this marketplace are checked on its consistency and its normality by using statistical software SPSS Statistic. The simulated marketplace is run 10, 30 and 50 times. By doing so, when the market is repeated with a relatively fewer runs, data consistency is checked. With these different numbers of runs, data collected are compared by using ANOVA test to check whether the closing prices are significantly different among these groups. In every run, 30 auctions, 180 standard bidders and 120 intelligent agents are generated by the system. More specifically, within the time t_0 to t_{max}, each auction will start and end according to their randomly assigned time constraints. Meanwhile, participants join different auctions based on their attributes. In this marketplace with the ratio used, standard bidders are distributed evenly across 30 auctions. Counter bidding process happens between standard bidders and intelligent agents until t_{max} is reached, then the market is said to have conducted a complete run.

Before performing the ANOVA test, two assumptions have to be verified, namely the normality of the data distribution and the homogeneity of variances. In the first verification, the hypotheses are given below:

H_0: The population means are equal among the groups of samples.

H_1: The population means are not equal among the groups of samples.

To check the distribution of the data collected, the Kolmogorov-Smirnov statistic with a Lilliefors significance level is used. From the results shown in Fig. 7, the significance levels of Kolmogorov-Smirnov (Sig.) in different runs are 0.200, 0.200 and 0.199 respectively, which are greater than 0.05. Therefore, null hypothesis is accepted. That is, the normality of data collected (closing prices) is assumed. In other words, data collected from the marketplace can be used to represent the actual scenario found in the real online auction houses since these data collected is distributed normally according to the SPSS analysis.

Next, the second assumption is checked. The Levene's test of homogeneity of variances is used for this purpose. However, from the result shown in Fig. 8, the second assumption cannot be verified ($p < 0.05$). Fortunately, SPSS does provide alternative approaches to verify the homogeneity of variances; they are the Brown-Forsythe and Welch procedures which can still be used to support the ANOVA test. From Fig. 9, the significance levels of Brown-Forsythe and Welch procedures are 0.537 and 0.670 respectively ($p > 0.05$). Hence, the homogeneity of variances is assumed.

Tests of Normality

	Number of Runs	Kolmogorov-Smirnov[a] Statistic	df	Sig.	Shapiro-Wilk Statistic	df	Sig.
Average Closing Price	10	.112	30	.200*	.960	30	.317
	30	.116	30	.200*	.967	30	.452
	50	.131	30	.199	.979	30	.801

*. This is a lower bound of the true significance.

a. Lilliefors Significance Correction

Fig. 7. Kolmogorov-Smirnov and Shapiro-Wilk statistic.

By using ANOVA test, a null hypothesis of "there is no significant difference among closing prices across different sets of samples" would be accepted if the significance level (Sig.) is greater than 0.05. From the results shown in Fig. 10, the null hypothesis is accepted since $F(2, 87) = 0.404$, $p = 0.669$ (Sig. value in ANOVA test) which is greater than 0.05. However, due to the violation of Levene's test of homogeneity of variances, therefore, the Brown-Forsythe *F*-ratio and Welch procedure are reported here. There is no significant difference among these closing prices across different sets of samples, since $F(2, 56.722) = 0.404$, $p > 0.05$ (Brown-Forsythe *F*-ratio) and $F(2, 53.278) = 0.629$, $p > 0.05$ (Welch procedure). In summary, from analyzing results of this ANOVA test, there is no significant difference found in the closing prices collected from various numbers of runs. Thus, in the following experiments, the simulations are run 10 times for different research purposes.

Test of Homogeneity of Variances

Average Closing Price

Levene Statistic	df1	df2	Sig.
12.387	2	87	.000

Fig. 8. Levene's test of homogeneity of variances.

Robust Tests of Equality of Means

Average Closing Price

	Statistic[a]	df1	df2	Sig.
Welch	.629	2	53.278	.537
Brown-Forsythe	.404	2	56.722	.670

a. Asymptotically F distributed.

Fig. 9. Brown-Forsythe and Welch procedures in ANOVA test.

ANOVA

Average Closing Price

	Sum of Squares	df	Mean Square	F	Sig.
Between Groups	6.087	2	3.044	.404	.669
Within Groups	655.808	87	7.538		
Total	661.895	89			

Fig. 10. ANOVA test.

4.3 Competition among heterogeneous standard bidders and homogeneous intelligent agents

In this experiment, 3 types of standard bidders are competing with the Heuristic agents simultaneously. Two simulations are conducted in this experiment. The first simulation is conducted to create the competition among standard bidders with assigned risk types and Heuristic agents. In the second simulation, the competition occurs among standard bidders with randomized risk types and Heuristic agents.

4.3.1 Experimental setup

In the first simulation, the numbers of standard bidders according to their different risk types are assigned. However, in the second simulation, the numbers of standard bidders with different risk attitudes are randomized by the system. The total number of buyers in the marketplace is always 300 and the proportion of standard bidders and intelligent agents is maintained in different runs. In a real auction marketplace, intelligent agents may observe their environment and obtain useful information such as the number of bidders. By running these two simulations, the agents' performance is tested when the numbers of standard bidders with different risk behaviors are known or when it is assumed wrongly. More specifically, there are 10 situations in every simulation and each situation is repeated 10 times. Every time a new situation is conducted, 10% of the standard bidders are replaced by the Heuristic agents until the last run, where 90% of the buyers are Heuristic agents. Intelligent agents of type Heuristic are selected to represent the intelligent agents because of their outstanding performance among the three types considered in this work (their performances are analyzed in Section 4.5.2). Nonetheless, there are always 30 auctions and 300 buyers found in the marketplace. Every auction generated has an active period of 100 time steps. Within this period of time, both standard bidders and Heuristic agents are competing to become the leading bidder in an auction.

4.3.2 Experimental results

a. Competition among Heterogeneous Standard Bidders with Assigned Risk Types and Heuristic Agents

In Fig. 11, it is observed that in all the situations where agents are found, their winner's utility is found higher than the other bidders' types. When agents were competing with multiple types of standard bidders in auction marketplace, they outperformed their counterparts by receiving higher intrinsic rewards. Besides that, generally, the rewards received by these Heuristic agents are increasing as more agents are found in the market.

Next, Heuristic agents successfully obtain the goods desired with lower prices compared to other bidders in the same market (Fig. 12). In addition, it is noticeable that the closing prices obtained by all winners' types seem to be converging towards Situation 9. It may be caused by the growing of the agent's population since Heuristic agents are capable on deciding the auction to be participated and the reasonable bids to be submitted. By doing so, they reduce bidding war with other participants but themselves in the market and as a result, the closing price of each auction is approximately distributed in a narrower range.

In Fig. 13, as the number of the standard bidder decreases, their number of winning auctions is also reduced. The two lines plotted in the same figure indicate the sums of auctions won by standard bidders and Heuristic agents. In this case, the number of auctions won by these agents is not as many as achieved by the standard bidders since these agents are equipped with the same strategy and are free to select their most promising auctions within the market, they may concentrate on several auctions while neglecting the less promising auctions. As a consequence, fewer auctions are won by the Heuristic agents.

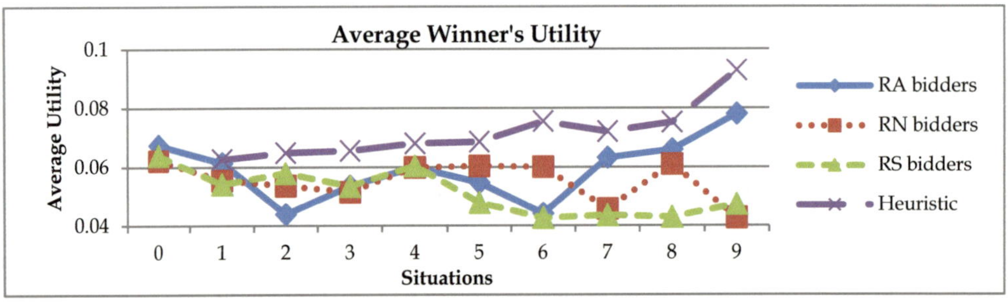

Fig. 11. Average winner's utility according to different winners' types.

Fig. 12. Average closing prices obtained by different winner's types.

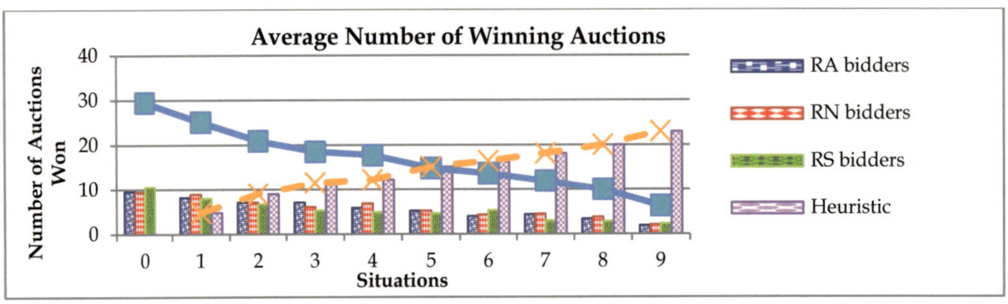

Fig. 13. Number of auctions won by different winner's types.

b. Competition among Heterogeneous Standard Bidders with Randomized Risk Types and Heuristic Agents

In Fig. 14, the winner's utility of the agents is fluctuated across the situations due to the irregularity of the numbers of standard bidders according to their risk behaviors that are found in the marketplace. When these numbers are unknown, Heuristic agents face the difficulty in tuning their bidding strategy appropriately. However, when comparison is made across the situations, the agents still received higher utilities in most of the situations.

Next, Fig. 15 shows the performance of different winners' types in terms of closing price. The most obvious observation is that the Heuristic agents successfully obtained their desired items with the lowest closing prices in all the situations considered. Besides that, the closing prices of all situations seem to be converging towards Situation 9. This is due to the growth of the agent population and thus reduces the bidding war among bidders. Consequently, the differences among closing prices of different winners' types are becoming smaller.

Lastly, as the population of agents is growing, they obtained more auctions compared to their counterparts (in Fig. 16). Nonetheless, the number of this achievement is not as high as the number achieved by those standard bidders. It may be due to the capability of Heuristic agents that are not restricted to any auctions. Therefore, they may select their best auctions to participate. In certain circumstances, some of the auctions are left without much attention from these agents. As a result, the number of winning auctions obtained by Heuristic agents is fewer than the auctions won by standard bidders.

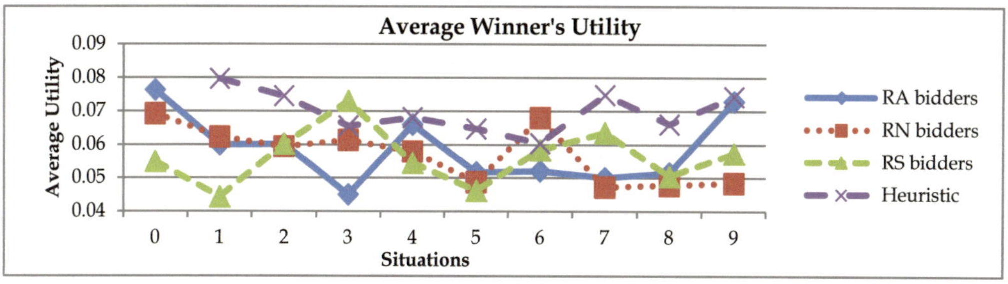

Fig. 14. Average winner's utility according to different winner's types.

Fig. 15. Average closing prices obtained by different winner's types.

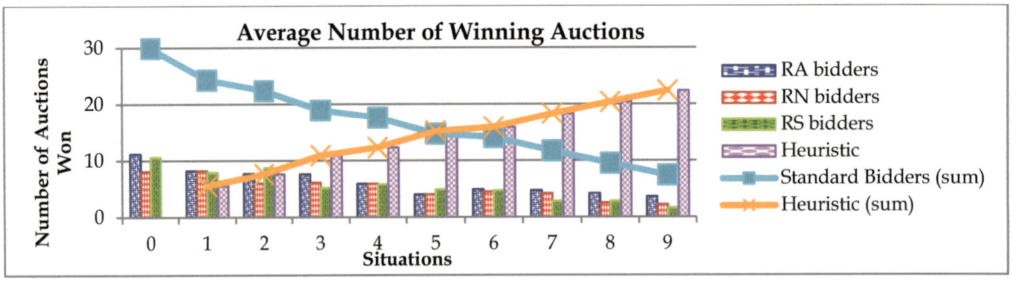

Fig. 16. Number of auctions won by different winner's types.

4.3.3 Summary of the experiment

Heuristic agents outperformed their competitors in obtaining goods desired while trying to keep the closing prices cheaper regardless of the correct assumption on the number of standard bidders based on their risk types. Therefore, from the bidders' point of view, it can be concluded that in general, by implementing agent technology, it improves their satisfaction in terms of the intrinsic saving values received and the auction closing prices. On the other hand, sellers' revenues are reduced in this experiment with finite auctions and participants since the auction closing prices are decreasing.

4.4 Competition among heterogeneous standard bidders and heterogeneous intelligent agents

In the next experiment, heterogeneous standard bidders and heterogeneous intelligent agents are generated in the same marketplace. In this experiment, performance of each winner's group is examined. Furthermore, the market economy is also evaluated.

4.4.1 Experimental setup

In this experiment, a simulation that involves both 3 types of standard bidders and 3 types of intelligent agents is considered. Besides the standard bidders and Heuristic agents, the Greedy agents and the Sniping agents are introduced. A Greedy agent is an agent that always participates in an auction with the lowest current bid. A Sniping agent is an agent that always targets on the auction that closes in the next possible moment. In this experiment, the competition occurs not only between standard bidders and intelligent agents, it occurs also within the groups of standard bidders and intelligent agents with different types. Hence, the auctions generated are increased to 90 and the total bidders are set to 900. Besides that, the number of situations used in this experiment is reduced to 4 as shown in Table 1. In this experiment, the focus is shifted from the advantages of using agents to the general market economy. Thus, fewer situations are considered. As multiple intelligent agents and standard bidders are located in a market, it would further simulate the real online auction marketplace where bidders may have different bidding behaviors or implement different bidder agents.

Situation	0	1	2	3
Standard Bidders	900	810	540	270
Intelligent Agents	0	90	360	630

Table 1. Proportion of participants in a marketplace

4.4.2 Experimental results

From Fig. 17, in all the situations analyzed, Greedy and Heuristic agents obtained higher winner's utility compared to other standard bidders. It may be credited to their bidding strategies which would lead them in suitable auctions and suggest an appropriate bid to be submitted. Sniping agents scored the lowest utility in all the situations because of its attitude of always search and snipe in the auctions that would close in the next time step. As a result, they may end up with paying higher prices when obtaining the items.

Next, the average number of winning auctions obtained by different groups of winners is illustrated in Fig. 18. First of all, standard bidders procured fewer items as more agents are located in the market. Besides that, Sniping agents successfully outperformed the other two types of agents in Situation 2 where 40% of the market participants are intelligent agents. It may indicate that sniping strategy is suitable to be used to obtain the items desired when agents' population is relatively smaller. Nonetheless, Heuristic agents performed outstandingly in Situation 3 with 20.6 auctions won on average. In all the situations analyzed, the overall closing numbers are 89.6, 89.4, 89.6 and 89.5 respectively. These numbers may not equal to 90 as some of the auctions are closed without winners (seller's reserve price is not met).

In Fig. 19, as more agents participate in an auction market, the closing price is decreasing. This can be seen from Situation 1 to Situation 3. There is an increase in closing price from Situation 0 to Situation 1. It may be explained as when more bidders' types are found in the market, it affects the competition that occurs within the market. Besides that, when comparison is made among the intelligent agents, it can be seen that Sniping agents pay more in obtaining the items desired. Their winning bids are greatly affected by the winning bids of other standard bidders. They always snipe in auctions at the very last possible moments. Thus, they have to submit higher bids to overbid the current leading bidders and it causes their closing prices to be the highest among the agents community.

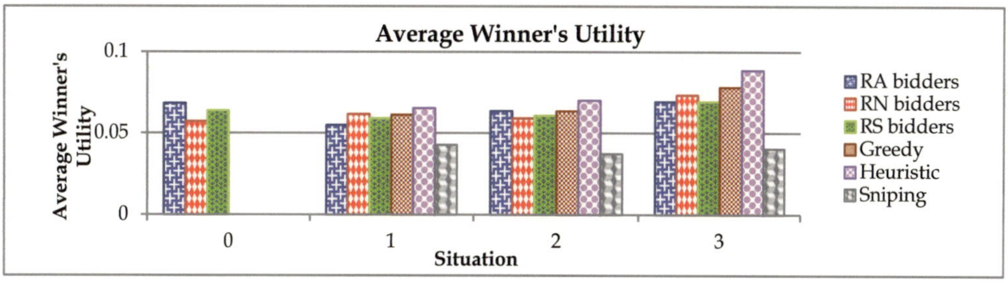

Fig. 17. Average winner's utility according to winner's types.

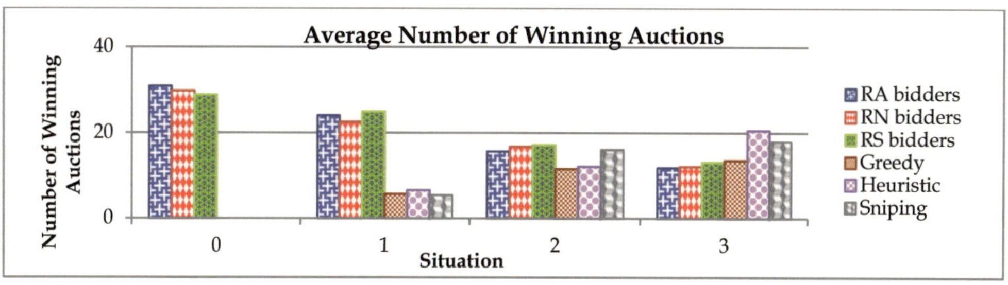

Fig. 18. Average number of winning auctions according to winner's types.

Fig. 19. Average closing price according to winner's types.

4.4.3 Summary of the experiment

Generally, in this experiment, the auction closing prices are decreasing as intelligent agents are involved in the market. Moreover, these agents successfully help their bidders to obtain items desired while trying to achieve greater saving. The Sniping agents do not perform well in obtaining desired goods while achieving greater saving as the other 2 types of agents. However, to those bidders who need the item required desperately, the Sniping agents may become one of their options since they would obtain the goods desired within a short period of time and the price paid is always within their private valuations. From the seller's perspective, they may prefer more standard bidders in their auctions than intelligent agents since more standard bidders increase their revenues gained from the auctions.

4.5 Special cases in simulated marketplace

In this experiment, two cases are considered and studied, a market that is fully populated by intelligent agents of single type is simulated and a market that is fully resided by multiple types of intelligent agents is analyzed. In both cases, besides the performances used in the previous experiments, the average CSR, is implemented. Due to the flexibility of agents, there may be an extreme case where several auctions are selected by all the agents while the rest of the auctions are left unattended or receive extremely few bids. Consequently, auctions with fewer bids may most probably close with low prices and vice-versa. Therefore, by using this CSR, it calculates the surplus ratio while minimizing the influence of the bids received by each auction and at the same time, it considers the median number of bids received across all the auctions generated.

4.5.1 Experimental setup

In the first simulation, a marketplace of 90 auctions is generated and the performances of 900 Heuristic agents are evaluated (homogeneous environment). Heuristic agents are selected in this homogeneous environment because of its outstanding performances compared to other types of agents implemented in this work (see Section 4.5.2 for its results). In the real auctioning world, it may be hard to find a market that is only resided by agents of single type. However, if a known strategy can guarantee a win in the auction with profit; eventually everyone will use the same strategy. This will lead to an environment similar to our case. Next, in the second simulation, 900 intelligent agents with various bidding strategies participate in 90 auctions generated (heterogeneous environment). The performances of these intelligent agents are analyzed and lastly a comparison between their performances and the performances of homogeneous agents is conducted.

4.5.2 Experimental results

Table 2 shows the various performances of intelligent agents in homogeneous environment and heterogeneous environment. On average, the homogeneous bidder agents recorded an average winner utility of 0.1318. Meanwhile, in the heterogeneous environment, Heuristic agents, Greedy agents and Sniping agents recorded average winning utilities of 0.1072, 0.0957 and 0.0391 respectively. A higher utility would mean a greater satisfaction for the winners since they receive higher intrinsic saving. The Sniping agents received the lowest utility because they ignored the auctions that are not closing soon but may return to them a better utility if they were winning in these auctions. When comparing the average utilities between Heuristic agents in Environment 1 and Environment 2, they received lower utility in heterogeneous environment as competition arises between groups of various agents.

Next, out of 90 auctions generated, 22.6 and 87.8 auctions on average are closed with winners in Environment 1 and 2 respectively. In Environment 1, since all of these Heuristic agents are equipped with the same strategy and are free to join any auction, they may end up bidding in similar auctions while neglecting the less promising auctions. Conversely, when various types of agents are populated in the market, they may select different auctions to join based on their strategies and thus encourage more successful trades. From Table 2, Heuristic agents obtained 53.56% of the items being auctioned (in Environment 2) in the market. This can be credited to their auction selection strategy and their bidding strategy that considers the available auction information. It is worth noticing that Sniping agents obtained more items than Greedy agents due to their sniping capability of giving insufficient time to their counterparts to react. Besides that, simply looking at the lowest current bid may lead the agents to jump from an auction with higher probability of winning to other more risky auctions.

Performances	Environment 1 A Market populated by Homogeneous Agents	Environment 2 A Market populated by Heterogeneous Agents		
	Heuristic	Greedy	Heuristic	Sniping
Average Winner's Utility	0.1318	0.0957	0.1072	0.0391
Average Winning Auction	22.6	16.5	48.2	23.1
Average CSR	0.1315	0.0817	0.1013	0.0110
Average Auction Closing Price	373.1478	344.6544		
Average Seller's Utility	0.3088	0.2497		
Average Median Number of Bids Received in a Completed Auction	26.8	14.7		

Table 2. Performances of Homogeneous and Heterogeneous Agents in a Market of 90 English Auctions Generated.

Furthermore, from Table 2 also, winners of type Heuristic received 0.1315 as their average CSR in homogeneous environment. On the other hand, Greedy agents, Heuristic agents and Sniping agents obtained 0.0817, 0.1013 and 0.0110 respectively as their average CSR in the heterogeneous environment. The Sniping agents received the lowest utility because they ignored the auctions that are not closing soon but may return to them a better utility if they were winning in these auctions. When comparing the average CSR between Heuristic agents in Environment 1 and 2, they received lower ratio in the latter environment as competition arises among groups of various agents (in Environment 2).

From Table 2 also, on average, each auction that is closed with a winner has a closing price of 373.1478 (in Environment 1) and 344.6544 (in Environment 2). In addition, from the sellers' perspective, they received 0.3088 and 0.2497 as their average utility in Environment 1 and Environment 2 respectively. This utility indicates the gross margin of the sellers. Lastly, on average, there are 26.8 bids (Environment 1) and 14.7 bids (Environment 2) received in every completed auction.

By comparing the results from both experiments, when homogeneous agents are competing with one another in a market, their average auction closing price is higher than the price in a market of heterogeneous agents. Those homogeneous agents with similar bidding strategy would most probably participate in few auctions and leave the rest of the auctions unattended. Therefore, the final closing price increases as the competition among buyers increases. It is supported by the average median number of bids submitted in a completed auction. This finding is also consistent with the suggestion in the work of Krishna (2002).

Even though a market with single type of agents produced a higher returned sellers' margin, in terms of the number of successful auctions, Environment 1 is worse than the Environment 2. Hence, if the average seller's profit is calculated based on the average auction closing price, the average seller's utility and the average number of traded auctions, the former market would generate 2604.1537 compared to the latter market that would produce 7556.0859. Based on the profit calculated, sellers may prefer heterogeneous bidder agents instead of homogeneous bidder agents as their auctions' participants since they bring more profit to sellers.

4.5.3 Summary of the experiment

In summary, in a market that is fully populated by homogeneous bidder agents, even though they obtained the highest average winner's utility and average CSR, they performed badly in terms of the number of winning auctions (25.11%). This finding is similar to the results obtained by Airiau and Sen (2003) and Byde (2002) which stated that multiple strategic buyers with the same strategy performed worse than their performance in situation where other types of bidders are present. Meanwhile, a market fully populated by heterogeneous bidder agents may achieve higher closing rate of 97.56% due to their various bidding strategies that led them to different auctions. Eventually, a healthier competitive environment was created. Moreover, sellers would prefer the participation of heterogeneous agents compared to homogeneous agents since it brings more sales and profit.

5. Conclusion

In this work, 3 distinct groups of standard bidders, namely the risk-averse, risk neutral and risk seeking bidders and 3 types of intelligent agents, namely the Greedy agents, the Heuristic agents and the Sniping agents are introduced to represent the potential buyers in the auctioning world according to their attributes. A market that is occupied by various standard bidders and intelligent agents would represent the real auction market where human bidders of different risk types and bidders who use intelligent agents as their representatives are competing with one another. From the empirical results, intelligent agents are capable in bringing more satisfaction to their owners if the correct agents are selected.

Besides that, markets that are fully dominated by homogeneous intelligent agents and fully dominated by heterogeneous intelligent agents are studied. It was clearly observed from the results obtained that a market that is occupied by intelligent agents of various types would benefit both sellers and buyers if the implementation of agent technology is unavoidable. Even though bidders may receive higher intrinsic saving value in homogeneous scenario, the chances of getting the desired items are greatly reduced. On the other hand, agent technology has been dominating the online auctioning world. Thus, sellers may welcome heterogeneous agents than homogeneous agents since the former encourages more trades than the latter.

There are still many aspects where this work does not cover where further researches can be explored. One of these areas would be the prediction capability. All the intelligent bidding strategies used in this research do not take into account the past historical data of the items being auctioned and therefore are not able to predict the auction closing prices. It would be useful if these intelligent agents are equipped with prediction capability in participating auctions. With the predicted closing price, agents can make better decision based on their private valuation and these predicted prices.

6. References

Airiau, S. & Sen, S. (2003). Strategic Bidding for Multiple Units in Simultaneous and Sequential Auctions. *Group Decision and Negotiation,* Vol. 12, pp. 397 - 413.

Anthony, P. & Jennings, N. R. (2003). Developing a Bidding Agent for Multiple Heterogeneous Auctions. *AMC Transactions on Internet Technology,* Vol. 3, No. 3, pp. 185 - 217.

Bierman, H. S. (1998). Uncertainty and Expected Utility, In: *Game Theory with Economic Applications,* Bierman, H. S. & Fernandez, L. (Eds.), pp. 207 - 238, Addison-Wesley Publishing Company, Inc., Boston.

Byde, A. (2002). A Comparison among Bidding Algorithms for Multiple Auctions, In: *Agent-Mediated Electronic Commerce 2002, LNAI 2531,* Padget, J.,Shehory, O., Parkes, D., Sadeh, N. & Wlash, W. E. (Eds.), pp.1 -16, Springer-Verlag, Berlin.

David, E., Rogers, A., Schiff, J., Kraus, S. & Jennings, N. R. (2005). Optimal Design of English Auctions with Discrete Bid Levels, *Proc. of the Sixth ACM Conf. on Electronic Commerce,* Vancouver, June 5 - 8, 2005.

Dignum, F. (2001). Agents, Markets, Institutions and Protocols. In: *Agent Mediated Elec. Commerce, LNAI 1991,* Dignum F. & Sierra C. (Eds.), pp. 98-114, Springer-Verlag, Berlin.

Ford, B. J., Xu, H. & Bates, C. K. Visual Specification of Layered Bidding Strategies for Autonomous Bidding Agents. *Journal of Computers,* Vol. 5, No. 6, pp. 940 - 950.

He, M., Jennings, N. R. & Prugel-Bennett, A. (2004). An Adaptive Bidding Agent for Multiple English Auctions: A Neuro-Fuzzy Approach, *Proc. of the IEEE International Conf. on Fuzzy Systems,* pp. 1519 - 1524, Budapest,Hungary, July 25 - 29, 2004.

He, M., Jennings, N. R. & Prugel-Bennett, A. (2006). A Heuristic Bidding Strategy for Buying Multiple Goods in Multiple English Auctions. *ACM Transactions on Internet Technology,* Vol. 6, No. 4, pp. 465 - 496.

Hu, W. & Bolivar, A. (2008). Online Auctions Efficiency: A Survey of eBay Auctions, *Proc. of the WWW 2008,* pp. 925 - 933, Beijing, 2008.

Jennings, N. R. & Wooldridge, M. (1998). Application of Intelligent Agents. In: *Agent Technology: Foundations, Applications and Markets,* Jennings, N. R. & Wooldridge, M. (Eds.), pp. 3-28, Springer-Verlag, Berlin.

Klemperer, P. (1999). Auction Theory: A Guide to the Literature, *Journal of Economic Survey.* Vol. 13, pp. 227 - 286.

Krishna, V. (2002). *Auction Theory,* Academic Press, San Diego.

Lee, Y. H. & Malmendier, U. (2007). The Bidder's Curse. *Working Paper 13699,* National Bureau of Economic Research, Cambridge.

Lim, D., Anthony, P. & Ho, C. M. (2007). Evaluating the Accuracy of Grey System Theory against Time Series in Predicting Online Auction Closing Price, *Proc. of the 2007 IEEE International Conf. on Grey Systems and Intelligent Services,* Nanjing, China, November 18 - 20, 2007.

Lim, D., Anthony, P., Ho, C. M. & Ng, K. W. (2008). Assessing the Accuracy of Grey System Theory against Artificial Neural Network in Predicting Online Auction Closing Price, *Proc. of the International Multi-Conf. of Engineers and Computer Scientists 2008 IMECS 2008,* Hong Kong, China, March 19 - 21, 2008.

Lin, C. S., Chou, S. Y., Chen, C. H., Ho, T. R. & Hsieh, Y. C. (2006). A Final Price Prediction Model for Online Auctions - A Neuro Fuzzy Approach, *Proc. of the Joint Conf. on Information Sciences 2006,* Kaohsiung, Taiwan, October 8 - 11, 2006.

Matthews, S. A. (1995). A Technical Primer on Auction Theory I: Independent Private Values, *Discussion Paper No. 1096,* Northwestern University, Evanston.

McAfee, R.P. & McMillan, J. 1987. Auctions and Bidding. *Journal of Economic Literature,* Vol. 25, No. 2, pp. 699-738.

Ockenfels, A. & Roth, A. E. (2002). The Timing of Bids in Internet Auctions: Market Design, Bidder Behavior, and Artificial Agents. *Journal Artificial Intelligent Magazine,* Vol. 23, No. 3, pp. 79 - 88.

Ockenfels, A. & Roth, A. E. (2006). Late and Multiple Bidding in Second Price Internet Auctions: Theory and Evidence Concerning Different Rules for Ending An Auction. *Games and Economic Behavior,* Vol. 55, pp. 297 - 320.

Park, S., Durfee, E. H. & Birmingham, W. P. (1999). An Adaptive Agent Bidding Strategy based on Stochastic Modeling, *Proc. of the 3rd Annual Conf. Autonomous Agents,* pp. 147 - 153, Washington, USA.

Roth, A. E. & Ockenfels, A. (2002). Last-Minute Bidding and the Rules for Ending Second-Price Auctions: Evidence from eBay and Amazon Auctions on the Internet. *American Economic Review,* Vol. 92, No. 4, pp. 1093 - 1103.

Talluri, K. T. & Ryzin, G. J. V. (2004). Auctions. In: *The Theory and Practice of Revenue Management 69,* Talluri, K. T. & Ryzin, G. J. V. (Eds.), pp.241 - 297, Springer, New York.

Watson, J. (2004). Risk and Incentives in Contracting. In: *Strategy: An Introduction to Game Theory,* Watson, J. (ed.), pp.245 - 255. W. W. Norton & Company, Inc., New York.

Wolfstetter, E. (1999). Auctions. In: *Topics in Microeconomics: Industrial Organization, Auctions and Incentives,* Wolfstetter E. (Ed), pp. 182 - 242. Cambridge University Press, Cambridge.

Yang, X. & Lu, T. (2007). Analysis of Bid Strategy with Game Theory in Auctions with a Buyout Price, *Proc. of the International Conf. on Service Systems and Service Management,* pp. 1 - 4.

Yuen, D. C. K., Byde, A. & Jennings, N. R. (2006). Heuristic Bidding Strategies for Multiple Heterogeneous Auctions, *Proc. of the 2006 Conf. on ECAI 2006: 17th European Conf.e on Artificial Intelligence,* pp. 300 - 304 Riva del Garda, Italy, August 26 - September 1, 2006.

4

Developing a Multi-Issue E-Negotiation System for E-Commerce with JADE

Bala M. Balachandran
Faculty of Information Sciences and Engineering
University of Canberra
Australia

1. Introduction

The rapid growth of the Internet, networking systems, and wireless and web technologies is stimulating more and more companies to provide e-commerce applications. E-commerce application developers have the problem of creating enterprise-wide and world-wide applications that must operate across corporations and continents of the world. Such e-commerce applications are difficult to produce with traditional software technologies. An agent is a software entity that applies Artificial Intelligence techniques to choose the best of actions to perform in order to reach a goal specified by the user. It should be proactive, flexible, dynamic and autonomous, and should act in an intelligent manner to the changes produced in its environment. A multi-agent system (MAS) may be defined as a collection of agents that communicate between themselves to coordinate their activities in order to be able to solve collectively a problem that could not be solved by an individual agent (Sycara, 1998; Wooldridge, 2010). Multi-agent systems have been shown to be suitable to domains with the following characteristics (Moreno and Isern, 2002):

- Knowledge is distributed in different locations.
- Several entities have to join their problem-solving abilities to be able to solve a complex problem.
- The problem in the domain may be decomposed into a set of different sub-problems, even if they have some kind of inter-dependencies.

There has been growing interest in the applications of agent and multi-agent systems to problems in the e-commerce domain (Paprzycki, 2004; Fasli, 2007; Balachandran, 2010). The characteristics and abilities of software agents have been found ideal to model problems in the e-commerce field. For example, intelligent agents can support buying and selling products and other services over the Internet for their customers. Other potential applications of agents in e-commerce include managing supply chains, conducting technical and market research, locating potential partners, negotiation, auctions, bargaining, voting protocols and coalition formation. Such agent-based e-commerce systems will deliver huge benefits to the businesses and to their customers.

In an e-commerce environment, agents should work collaboratively, resolve conflicts and come to a common conclusion to a shared problem. The agents can be friendly (in which they work together in a team), or they could be opposed to each other (in which they work against each other). Either way, multi-agent systems highlight the social complexities and capabilities of software agents (Alem et al., 2002). When considering an agent-oriented view of e-commerce, it becomes evident that most problems involve multiple agents. Having multiple agents in a system increases its complexity because of the need for the agents to interact with each other and collaborate effectively in the common environment. These interactions can be simple such as those made between a client and a web server, or they can be composed of rich social interactions such communication, collaboration and negotiation as required (Paprzycki et al, 2004).

One of the key problems in implementing an agent-based e-commerce system is the question of what agents are necessary, how they should communicate, what strategy is required, and how it should be implemented. In this chapter, we have attempted to address these questions in the context of a multi-agent system for providing personalised buying and selling services. This chapter is organised as follows. First, we review agent-based negotiation and some related works. We then present our proposed negotiation model, discussing its ability to handle customer preferences based on multiple issues. We describe the model in terms of the negotiation object, the negotiation protocol and the negotiation strategy. Then we describe details of a prototype system we have developed using JADE and the Eclipse platform. Finally, we present our concluding remarks and discuss our future work.

2. Agent-based negotiation

Negotiation is defined as a process in which two or more parties with different criteria, constraints and preferences jointly reach an agreement on the terms of a transaction (Paprzcki et al., 2004). For agents to be involved in negotiation, we need to consider the following:

- Negotiation protocols (rules) governing interactions
- Negotiation issues (objects) over which agreement must be made
- Reasoning model (mechanisms used for negotiation) depends upon the first two points

The process of bargaining is a type of negotiation which occurs between a single buyer and a single seller. Buyers and sellers bargain with each other to reach a solution which is mutually acceptable. In the traditional sense, bargaining happens between a seller and customer. The seller is skilled in the arts of bargaining and will attempt to entice the buyer into making a purchase where there is more profit for the seller. In a bargaining process, the buyer and the seller exhibit different behaviours and attributes. (Sheng 2004). In a buyers' point of view, they would experience a sense of satisfaction at getting a deal even though the price achieved may not be the lowest possible. Generally, price may not be the most important factor for the buyer. From the sellers' point of view, they can make use of the extra information they have about the supply and demand of a particular item when setting its price. They are able to better customise their products to the individual needs of customers, hence giving a greater sense of satisfaction to their customers.

Agents provide an ideal platform for bargaining because the agent oriented model is inherently responsive to a rapidly changing environment, is dynamic in nature and autonomous in its actions. Agents are also designed to meet their design objectives. In an agent-based bargaining model, there would be specialised agents which carry out the tasks of parties involved in a bargaining process. There would be a buyer, who is trying to get the best combination of a few different variables (e.g. Price, quality, delivery time). The seller would be the bargaining agent who would try to entice the buyer into buying a product at the highest possible revenue. In order to reach a mutual agreement in a bargaining situation involves finding an acceptable solution for both the buyer and seller. This implies that the buyer's behaviours and attributes should also be considered. These behaviours and attributes could be modelled into a software agent who will then commence in the bargaining process. Figure 1 shows a typical bargain protocol between two agents.

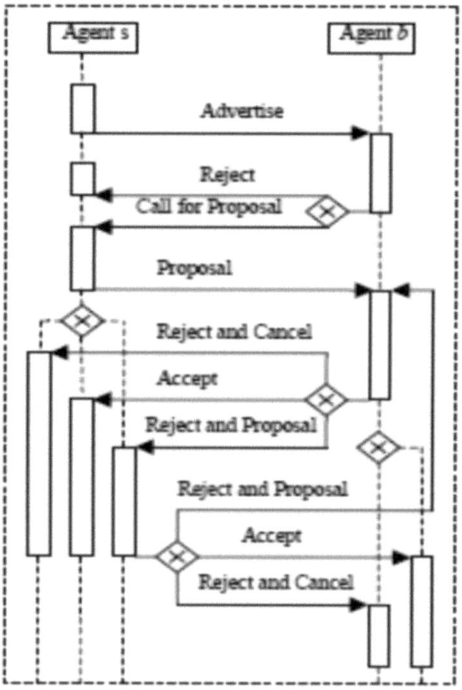

Fig. 1. A typical bargain protocol between two agents

2.1 Related work

There is a body of work on the applications of agent and multi-agent systems for electronic commerce. Recent advances in agent technology have promoted the development of intelligent e-commerce systems (Balachandran, 2010, 2011). Such systems are built upon the foundations of agent technology with a strong emphasis on the agent collaboration and negotiation capabilities. There have been several models developed for negotiation. Some examples include bargaining, fuzzy reasoning, and argumentation (Wooldridge, 2009). Broadly, these approaches have stemmed from two distinct fields of research: Game theory and artificial intelligence (Paprzycki 2004).

There have been many different mechanisms proposed for automated negotiations in literature and they each have their own advantages and drawbacks. Merlat (1999) discusses the potential of agent-based multiservice negotiation for e-commerce and demonstrates a decentralized constraint satisfaction algorithm (DCSP) as a means of multiservice negotiation. Badica et al (2006) present a rule based mechanism for agent price negotiation. They discuss the goals/challenges of developing an automated negotiation system for eCommerce. Sheng (2004) presents work that offers customers online business-to-customer bargaining service. Lai, Sycara, & Li (2007) present a Pareto optimal model for automated multi-attribute negotiations.and discuss issues, challenges and view points in agent-mediated eCommerce. Lomuscio et al (2003) provide an insightful overview of the existing research efforts on negotiation and describe a classification scheme for negotiation in electronic commerce. Liu and Feng (2007) presents work on e-commerce oriented automated negotiation based on FIPA Interaction Protocol Specification.

3. Modelling agent negotiation with multiple issues

If the bargaining process was centred over a single issue (such as the price), then it is relatively straightforward. The buyer will search for the lowest price offered for an item of their choice. Once the lowest price is found, that is the optimal solution to the problem. However, in real world bargaining situations, it is never this simple. There are always multiple issues to consider such as the price, quality, quantity, warranty, delivery date etcetera. As the number of issues being considered increases, so does the complexity of the negotiation (Yoshikawa 2006).

In this section we present a multi-issue negotiation model for e-commerce in which agents autonomously negotiate multi-issue terms of transactions in a bargaining environment. We use three agents in our model: a buyer agent, a seller agent, and a facilitator agent. The seller agent allows a seller to determine his negotiation strategies for selling merchandise. Similarly, the buyer agent allows a buyer to determine his negotiation strategies for buying merchandise. The facilitator agent serves to handle the negotiation strategies for both the buyer and the seller agents. In our approach, agents' preferences are expressed in fuzzy terms. The application domain for our prototype implementation is buying and selling laptop computers.

The negotiation model we have chosen for our study is illustrated in Figure 2. In this model, issues within both the buyer's request and the seller's offer can be split into hard constraints and soft constraints. Hard constraints are issues that have to be necessarily satisfied in the final agreement, whereas soft constraints represent issues they are willing to negotiate on. We utilise a facilitator agent which collects information from bargainers and exploits them in order to propose an efficient negotiation outcome.

The negotiation module consists of three components: negotiation object, decision making model and negotiation protocol. The negotiation object is characterised by a number of attributes for which the agents can negotiate. The decision making model consists of an assessment part which evaluates an offer received and determines an appropriate action, and an action part which generate and send a counter-offer or stop the negotiation. The assessment part is based on the fact that different values of negotiation issues are of different value for negotiating agents. We model the value of negotiating issues by scoring functions (Kurbel et al., 2004). The bigger the value of a scoring function for a certain value of an issue is, the more suitable is this value for a negotiating agent.

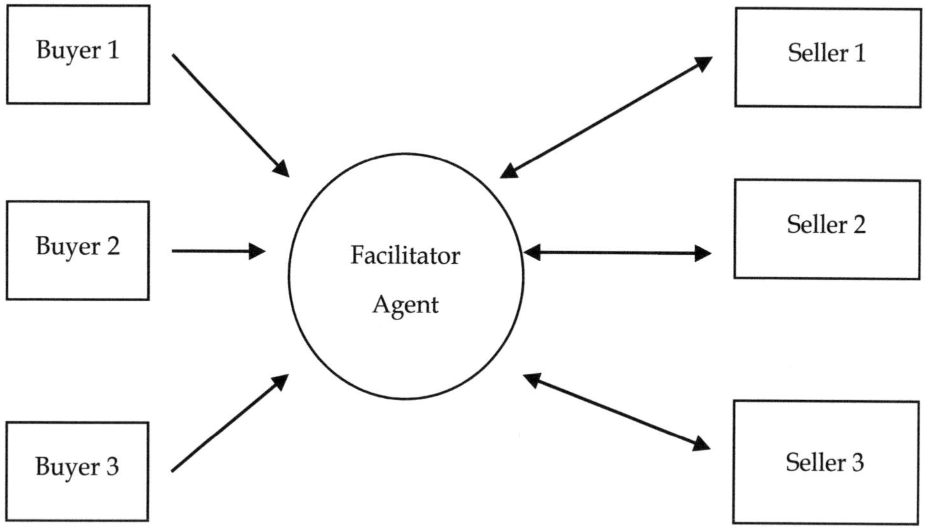

Fig. 2. One-to-many negotiation scheme

3.1 Scoring functions

The scoring functions represent private information about their preferences regarding the negotiation issues. This information is not given to other participants in the negotiation process. A scoring function is defined by four values of a negotiation issue. They are the minimal, maximal, optimum minimal and optimum maximal as illustrated in Figure 3 below:

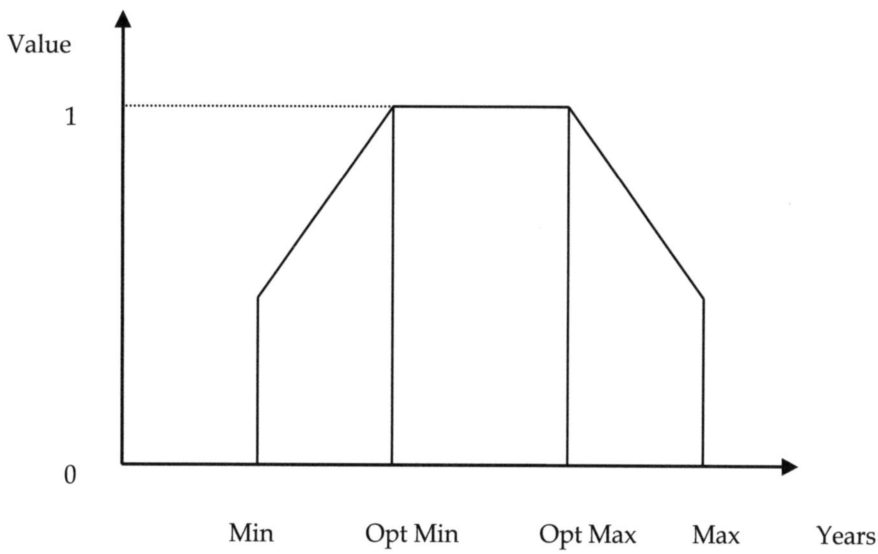

Fig. 3. Scoring Function for negotiation issue “number of years warranty"

We also consider the fact that different negotiation issues are of different importance for each participant. To model this situation, we introduce the weighting factor representing the relative importance that a participant assigns to an issue under negotiation.

During negotiation, the value of an offer received is calculated using two vectors: a vector-valued offer received by an agent and a vector of relative importance of issues under negotiation. The value of an offer is the sum of the products of the scoring functions for individual negotiation issues multiplied by their relative importance.

3.2 Pareto optimality

In order to find the most optimal solution to a multi-dimensional problem, the Pareto algorithm can be used to determine if one alternative is better than another (Keeny and Raiffa, 1976). A buyers Pareto optimal solution would be quite different to the Pareto optimal solution of a seller. In fact, they are likely to be the opposite. The negotiation process will attempt to find a mutually acceptable situation for both buyer and seller. This is likely to be in between the buyer's and the seller's Pareto optimal solutions. Figure 4 depicts a Pareto graph to show how two attributes (Price and Quality) are being optimized. The blue dots are where there are possible solutions and the red line shows where the optimal solution set is. All the possible solutions are covered under the red line. In this case, as you go towards the edges of the graph the item is being optimised. So to optimize price, one would have to go to the far right of the graph. This would have different meaning for buyer and seller because the buyer would consider the optimal price to be the lowest price, but the seller would consider the optimal price to be the highest possible price.

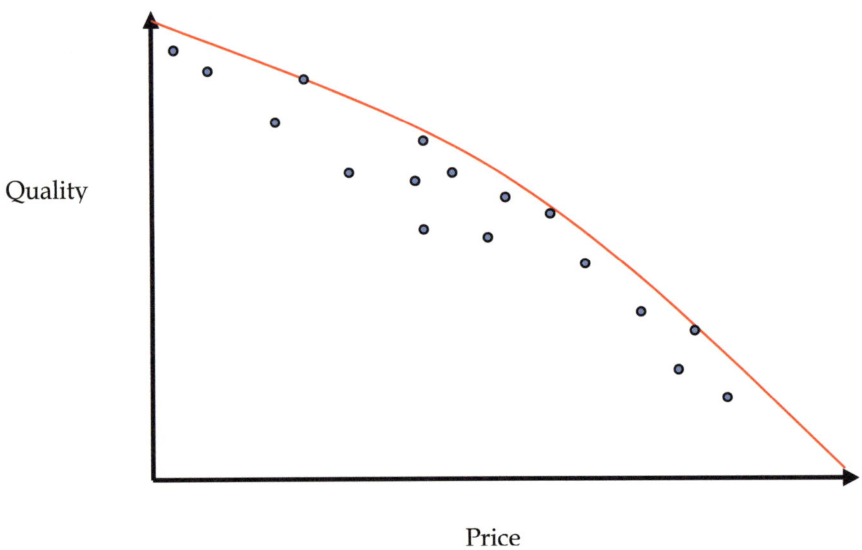

Fig. 4. Pareto Optimality Graph

3.3 The negotiation protocol

The negotiation facilitator receives this request and registers the customer. Once this is done, the negotiation process can begin with the suppliers. The negotiation facilitator requests the suppliers to provide offers conforming to the restrictions imposed by the customer agent. Please note that each restriction has an importance rating (0% to 100%), which means there is some leniency in the restrictions imposed by the customer. For example if the customer wants the colour Red, but provides an importance rating of 50%, it is quite lenient and the negotiation facilitator will request suppliers to make offers for a range of different colours. The negotiation facilitator and suppliers go through several rounds of negotiation until they reach the maximum number of rounds. Then the best offer (optimal set) is sent back to the customer agent. The customer agent then displays the results of the negotiation process to the end user who is ultimately responsible for making the decision on which item to buy.

3.4 The negotiation strategy

The facilitator's strategy is to gather a set of offers from the listed suppliers which satisfy the customer's wishes. Each offer is compared with the last offer by using a Pareto optimality algorithm. The facilitator has a utility algorithm which shows how good a particular offer is, this facilitator may modify the customers preferences (those which have an importance rating of less than 100%) in order to find other offers which may satisfy the user's needs. Once the set of optimal results are obtained, it is sent back to the customer agent.

The buyer's strategy is one which aims to maximise their profits on the goods sold to customers. They would also like to sell the goods as fast as possible, but at the highest possible price. The supplier does not want any old stock which cannot be sold.

3.5 The negotiation process

The negotiation process begins with registered buyers and sellers and a single facilitator. The seller sends a list of all items for sale to the facilitator. These items are registered for sale and available for all the buyers to bargain on and purchase. The buyer then registers with the facilitator and sends all their preferences. Once the preferences have been received by the facilitator, the negotiation process can begin between the facilitator and the supplier:

1. Facilitator runs the Pareto optimality algorithm to remove any sub-optimal solutions
2. Facilitator runs the Scoring function to get the item with the highest utility.
3. This item with the highest utility is selected as the negotiation item and set as the base item with all its properties (price, hard drive space etc.)
4. The item's properties are changed so that the property with the highest importance factor is increased. If importance factor of price was highest, it would be reduced by 10%. If the importance factor of the hard drive space or any other property was the highest, then it would be increased by 10%
5. This is sent to the supplier to see if they agree with the properties
6. This counter offer is received by the supplier who has a negotiable threshold amount (set to 10% by default) by which they are willing to negotiate on the items properties

a. If the negotiable threshold is not crossed, the counter offer is agreed to and sent back to the facilitator

b. If the negotiable threshold has been crossed, then check by how much. This difference is added to the price. If the threshold is crossed by 5%, then the price is increased by 5% and sent back to the facilitator
7. When the facilitator receives this offer, it calculates the utility of the offer and if it is greater, then it becomes the new base item. The next round of bargaining begins (back to step 4)
8. The bargaining process happens for a fixed number of rounds, 4 by default

4. An overview of the JADE platform

JADE (Java Agent Development Framework) is a software environment fully implemented in JAVA language aiming at the development of multi-agent systems that comply with FIPA specifications. This framework is provided free of charge by TILabs (http://jade.tilab.com/) and runs entirely on the Java runtime environment. JADE provides many of the base classes required for agent based software development (Bellifemine, Caire, and Greenwood, 2007). Some of them are:

- Agent
- Behaviour
- ACL Messaging
- Ontology

One goal of JADE is to simplify development while ensuring standard compliance through a comprehensive set of system services and agents. It provides the following mandatory components for agent's management:

- AMS (Agent Management System), which besides providing white page services as specified by FIPA, it also plays the role of authority in the platform.
- DF (Directory Facilitator) provides yellow pages services to other agents.
- ACC (Agent Communication Channel) which provides a Message Transport System (MTS) and is responsible for sending and receiving messages on an agent platform.

Eclipse is the IDE (Integrated development environment) commonly used to develop the JADE application. It is quite easy to integrate Eclipse with JADE so that when the agent application is executed, it runs JADE and deploys the Agent into the runtime environment. Figure 5 shows a screen dump of the development environment using Eclipse and JADE.

In the following subsections we discuss the various steps involved in developing a multi-agent system using JADE.

4.1 Creating agents

Creating a JADE agent is as simple as defining a class that extends the jade.core. Agent class and overriding the default implementation of the methods that are automatically invoked by the platform during the agent lifecycle, including SetUp and TakeDown (). Consistent with the FIPA specifications, each agent instance is identified by an 'agent identifier'. In JADE an agent identifier is represented as an instance of the jade.core.AID class. The getAID () method of the Agent class allows retrieval of the local agent identifier.

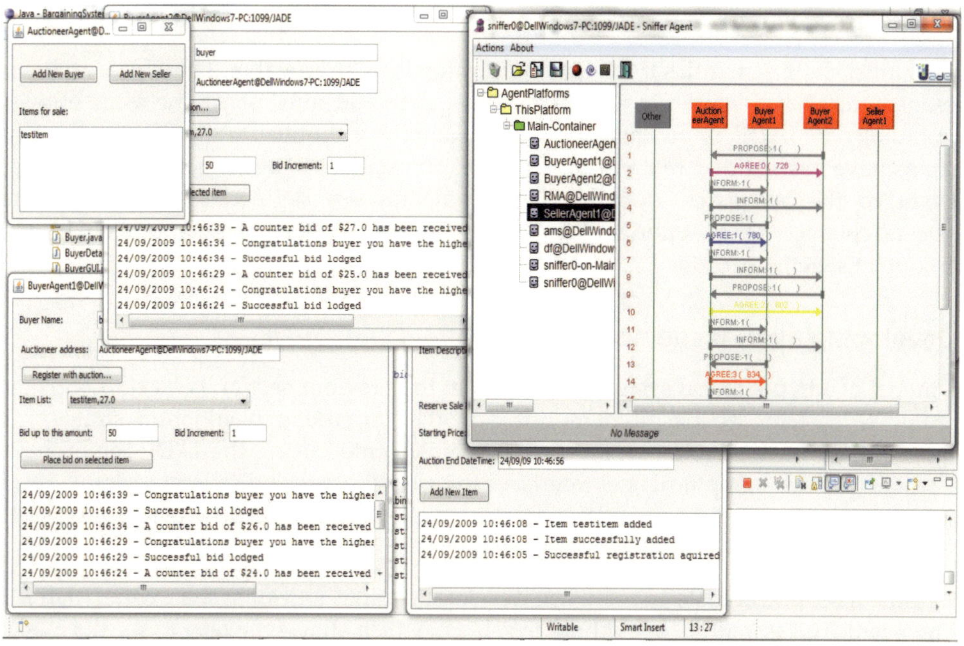

Fig. 5. The Development environment using Eclipse and JADE

4.2 Defining agent tasks

In JADE, behaviour represents a task that an agent can carry out and is implemented as an object of a class that extends jade.core.behaviours.Behaviour. Each such behaviour class must implement two abstract methods. The action () method defines the operations to be performed when the behaviour is in execution. The done () method returns a Boolean value to indicate whether or not a behaviour has completed and is to be removed from the pool of behaviours an agent is executing. To make an agent execute the tasks represented by a behaviour object, the behaviour must be added to the agent by means of the add Behaviour () method of the Agent class.

4.3 Agent discovery process

The JADE platform provides a yellow pages service which allows any agent to dynamically discover other agents at a given point in time. A specialised agent called the DF (Directory Facilitator) provides the yellow pages service in JADE. Using this service any agent can both register (publish) services and search for (discover) services.

4.4 Agent communication

Agent communication is probably the most fundamental feature of JADE and is implemented accordance with the FIPA specifications. The JADE communication paradigm is based on asynchronous message passing. Each agent is equipped with an incoming message box and message polling can be blocking or non-blocking. A message in JADE is implemented as an object of the jade.lang.acl.ACLMessage object and then calling the send () method of the Agent class.

4.5 Defining ontologies

Agents must share semantics if the communication is to be effective. Therefore, exchanged messages must have written in a particular language and must share the same ontology. An ontology in JADE is an instance of the jade.content.onto.Ontology class to which schemas have been added that define the types of predicates, agent actions and concepts relevant to the addressed domain. These schemas are defined as instances of the PredicateSchema, AgentAction Schema and ConceptSchema classes included in the jade.content.schema package.

5. Developing multi-issue negotiation system with JADE

The model of a hypothetical system developed in the previous section is used to implement a prototype system capable of demonstrating the bargaining negotiation strategy. The proposed multi-issue negotiation system was implemented using the JADE environment. The system provides graphical user interfaces for users (buyers and sellers) to define scoring functions, weighting factors, negotiation tactics. It also has a customer management system for the system administrator.

One of the most useful tools to use when developing a multi-agent system with JADE is the Sniffer agent. This is another agent built into JADE which allows the user to see the message interactions taking place in real time. It can be seen in Figure 6 below that the interactions depicts the type of message, the sender and receiver and when it was sent within the lifetime of the system. If more information is required about any of the ACL messages, the user can double click the specific arrows and it will display full details.

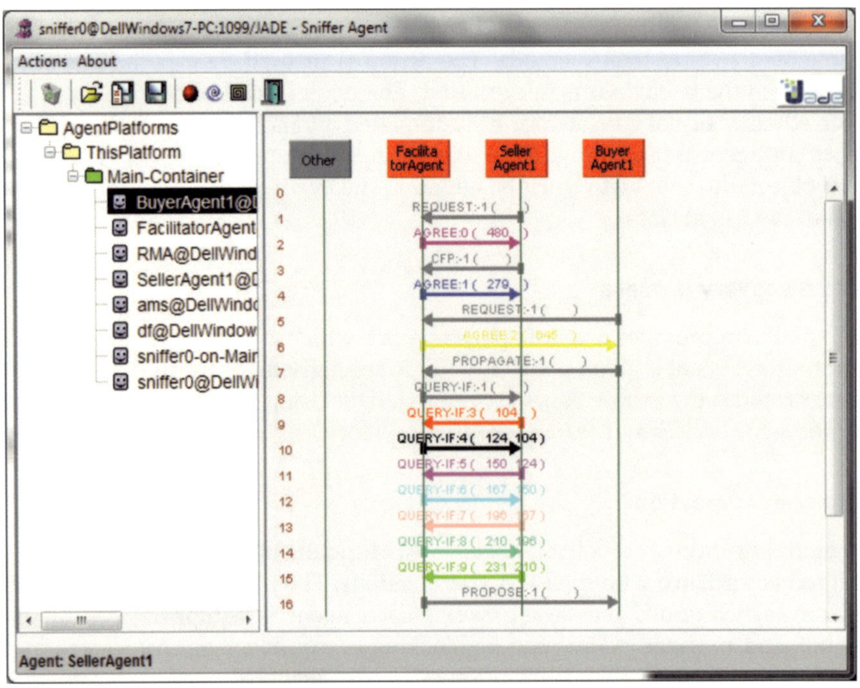

Fig. 6. A screenshot of the JADE sniffer agent

5.1 A case study

When someone wishes to buy a computer/laptop, they have to go through a process to determine which one is best suited to their needs and requirements. One of the buyer's requirements could be that the price is below $1500. Likewise the following could be the set of requirements for the buyer:

- 15.6" screen
- 500GB hard drive
- 4 USB ports
- Brand quality

For each of these requirements, there is a priority associated which shows how much the importance of fulfilling that particular requirements is for the buyer. For example, the laptop must be below or equal to $1500. This is not a negotiable item, so its importance factor is 100%. The hard drive, however, can be of a lower size as long as there is a reasonable adjustment in the other requirements of the laptop. For example, if the laptop has less than 500GB hard drive, then price of the product should be less than one which has a 500GB hard drive. In these ways, there are many different rules which assist the user in determining the value of one deal compared to another. The buyer is basically calculating optimality of one solution/possibility compared to another. The goal is to maximise the optimality so that there is no other solution which is of better suitability to the buyer.

In order for a customer with basic knowledge of computer systems to choose the best available computer, the buyer needs to do comprehensive research online and at electronic stores. There is often conflicting and confusing information on display to consumers. Because it is such a daunting experience to go through all the computers for sale and compare one to the other purely on a factual level, consumers can often make purchases which do not optimise the money they are spending.

Computer systems make decisions purely based on the facts available to it. They are able to sift through large amounts of data and use complex algorithms to compare and contrast the different options for the user. All this should be done based on the 'value' to the customer, rather than just the lowest price. Price is only one of the factors which influence a buyer's decision on whether or not to make a purchase. There are many other factors which must be considered. The majority of computer systems currently work based on the concept that a lower priced good is always better than a higher priced good. Web sites like EBay and Amazon allows the user to negotiate the price so that they may achieve the highest value. However, buying a product is rarely a black and white decision based purely on money. Admittedly the price is a very important factor, but it is definitely not the only factor which should be considered.

In this chapter, we present a prototype system which will demonstrate the use of multi-issue negotiation in order to achieve the optimal value for the user. So far, the buyer has been of our main concern, but similar considerations can be made for the seller in order to increase their revenue.

5.2 Agents in the system

This section will describe the agent screens as developed as part of the prototype multi agent system. There are three agents in total. Although there can be more than one instance of the buyer and seller, there can only be one instance of the facilitator running at any one time. This is a limitation on the system imposed to reduce the complexity of the application. The main aspect of the system that this project is interested is the negotiation component. The prototype system implements multi-attribute bargaining.

5.2.1 Buyer agent

The buyer agent is designed to get the preferences from the user, register with the facilitator and then receive the results of the negotiation process. From the point the user clicks on search, there is no interaction between this agent and the end user, until the negotiation results are returned. Using the buyer agent's screen , the end user selects their preference values and importance factors. This information is used by the facilitator during the bargaining process. Figure 7 shows the buyer agent screen.

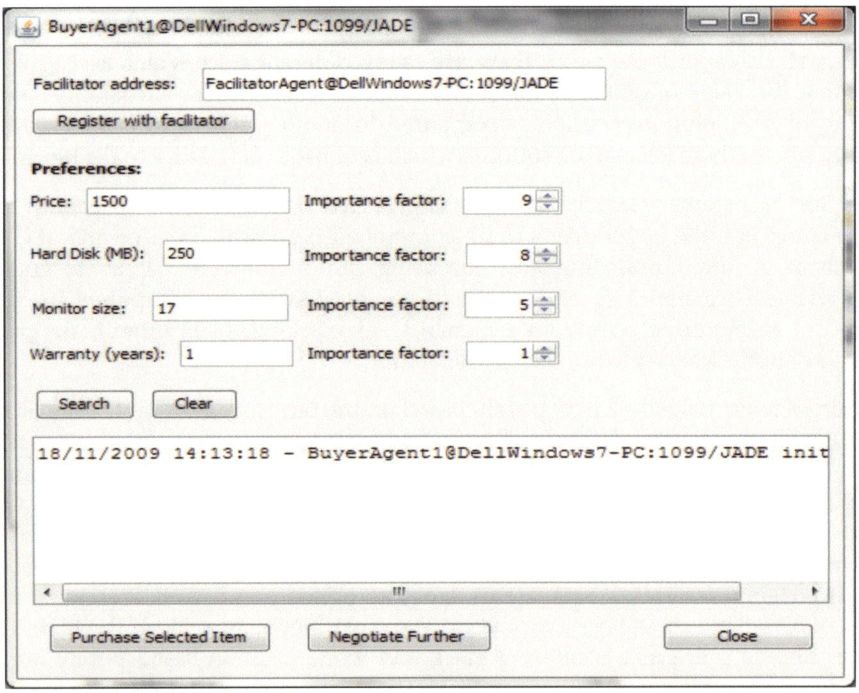

Fig. 7. The buyer agent screen

5.2.2 Facilitator agent

The facilitator agent receives registration requests from both the buyer and seller and then process the request (either accepts or denies the registration request). Once all the information for a round of negotiation is available, the facilitator looks after the bargaining process with the supplier. Once the maximum number of negotiation rounds has been completed, the facilitator sends the best offer back to the buyer.

5.2.3 Seller agent

The seller agent is responsible for registering with the facilitator and sending a list of sale items which are available. This agent also manages the counter offers received from the facilitator. The agent has a threshold limit as to how much it is able to negotiate. All offers where it needs to negotiate more incur an increase in the price of the good.

5.3 The negotiation object

The negotiation object in our model is the item which is being negotiated upon. This item, A, has several properties and each property has a name and value. For the purposes of this project, the name is a string and the value is an integer whole number. These item details are read in by the agents and the properties manipulated during the negotiation process. Figure 8 shows an example XML document showing a sale Item and its properties.


```
- <SaleItems>
  - <SaleItem>
      <SaleItemName>Dell Inspiron</SaleItemName>
      <Description>Laptop with screen</Description>
      <MinumumSellPrice>1500.0</MinumumSellPrice>
      <StartingBidPrice>1000.0</StartingBidPrice>
      <AuctionFinishDateTime>02/11/09 3:00:00</AuctionFinishDateTime>
    - <Properties>
      - <Property>
          <Name>ScreenSize</Name>
          <Value>20</Value>
        </Property>
      - <Property>
          <Name>HardDisk</Name>
          <Value>200</Value>
        </Property>
      - <Property>
          <Name>Warrenty</Name>
          <Value>2</Value>
        </Property>
      </Properties>
    </SaleItem>
  + <SaleItem>
  </SaleItems>
```


Fig. 8. A sale item representation in XML

5.4 The negotiation protocol

The negotiation facilitator receives this request and registers the customer. Once this is done, the negotiation process can begin with the suppliers. The negotiation facilitator requests the suppliers to provide offers conforming to the restrictions imposed by the customer agent. Please note that each restriction has an importance rating (0% to 100%), which means there is some leniency in the restrictions imposed by the customer. For example if the customer wants the colour Red, but provides an importance rating of 50%, it is quite lenient and the negotiation facilitator will request suppliers to make offers for a range of different colours. The negotiation facilitator and suppliers go through several rounds of negotiation until they reach the maximum number of rounds. Then the best offer (optimal set) is sent back to the customer agent. The customer agent then displays the results of the negotiation process to the end user who is ultimately responsible for making the decision on which item to buy.

5.5 The negotiation strategy

The facilitator's strategy is to gather a set of offers from the listed suppliers which satisfy the customer's wishes. Each offer is compared with the last offer by using a Pareto optimality algorithm. The facilitator has a utility algorithm which shows how good a particular offer is, and the facilitator may modify the customers preferences in some circumstances (those which have an importance rating of less than 100%) in order to find other offers which may satisfy the user's needs. Once the set of optimal results are obtained, it is sent back to the customer agent.

The seller's strategy is one which aims to maximise their profits on the goods sold to customers. They would also like to sell the goods as fast as possible, but at the highest possible price. The supplier does not want any old stock which cannot be sold.

6. Summary and conclusions

In this chapter, we have described a multi-issue negotiation protocol which allows agents to follow a process, in order to end up with an optimal decision. Further we have described design and implementation of automated negotiations in an e-commerce modelling multi-agent system. We have implemented a working prototype of the system using the JADE and ECLIPSE platforms. JADE is very easy to learn and use. Moreover we found that JADE is quite suitable for developing multi-agent systems as it supports many agent concepts such as agent communication, protocol, behaviour and ontology. We have done some evaluation to investigate the satisfaction of using the prototype system. The System has met the functionalities expected and has been tested for the domain of buying a laptop computer for given user preferences. The concepts and models utilised in this chapter are very promising for the future e-commerce applications.

There are a number of areas of further investigation. We would like to compare our negotiation strategy with other decision theoretic approaches to determine the relative strengths and weaknesses of these methods. The use of scoring function is purely number based and the users' preferences currently have to be numerated into a number value indicating their importance. This may not be possible in many situations. We intend to use fuzzy techniques to model user preferences. Furthermore the current negotiation strategy is heavily based upon the views of the buyer, and attempts to negotiate a deal with the supplier which would see greater value for the buyer. A better supplier strategy could be implemented which could also take multiple issues into consideration (such as stock items for sale, and time before stock replacement).

In conclusion, there are opportunities for future improvements and further development in this area of e-commerce. The current system focuses on utility based bargaining on different items for sale. It aims to provide the best possible deal for the customer. Work could be done in the future to further enhance the model and the system to incorporate new tools and techniques used in the electronic marketplace. In the future, we would like to extend our work by implementing more sophisticated individual strategies and knowledge sharing ability between agents. Another important area of extension is the ability to handle non-linear scoring functions to represent agents' preferences.

7. Acknowledgment

We would like to thank Mr Tauhid Tayeb, for his efforts in implementing the prototype system described in this chapter.

8. References

Alem, L, Kowalczyk, R, and Lee, M.R. (2002). Supporting Electronic Negotiation for Intelligent Trading, Idea Group Publishing

Badica, C., Badita, A., & Ganzha, M. (2006). Implementing rule-based mechanisms for agent-based price negotiation. ACM, 96-100

Balachandran, B.M, Gobbin, R, and Sharma, D. (2011). Development of a Multi-Issue Negotiation System for E-Commerce, KES-IDT'2011, Athens, Greece

Balachandran, B.M, Tayeb, T, Sharma, D, and Mohammadian, M. (2010). An Implementation of a Multi-Attribute Negotiation Protocol for E-Commerce, KES-IDT'2010, Baltimore, Maryland, USA

Bellifemine F, Caire G, and Greenwood, D. (2007) Developing Multi-Agent Systems with JADE, John Wiley & Sons, UK

Fasli, M. (2007). "Agent Technology for e-Commerce", John Wiley and Sons, UK

FIPA (2006) The Foundation for Intelligent Physical Agents. See http://www.fipa.org/

JADE: Java Agent Development Framework: http://jade.tilab.com

Keeny,R. and Raiffa,H.(1976). Decisions with Multiple Objectives: Preferences and Value Tradeoffs, John Willey & Sons

Kurbel, K., Loutchko, I, and Teuteberg, F (2004). FuzzyMAN: An agent-based electronic market place with a multilateral negotiation protocol, G. Lindemann et al. (Eds), MATES 2004, LNAI 3187, pp.126-140, 2004

Lai, G., Sycara, K., & Li, C. (2007). A Pareto Optimal Model for Automated Multi-attribute Negotiations. IFAAMAS

Liu, K. and Feng, Y. (2007). E-Commerce Oriented Automated negotiation Based on FIPA Interaction Protocol Specification, Proceedings of the Sixth International Conference on machine Learning and Cybernetics, Hong Kong, 19-22 August 2007

Lomuscio, A.R., Wooldridge, M, and Jennings, N.R. (2003). A Classification Scheme for Negotiation in Electronic Commerce, Group Decision and Negotiation, Kluwer Academic Publishers, 12:31-56

Merlat, W. (1999). An Agent-Based Multiservice Negotiation for Ecommerce, BT technical Journal, Vol 17 No 4 pp:168-175

Moreno, A and Isern, D. (2002). Accessing distributed health-care services through smart agents, Proceedings of the 4th IEEE International Workshop on Enterprise Networking and Computing in the Health Care Industry, Nancy, France, pp34-41

Paprzycki M et al., (2004) Implementing Agents Capable of Dynamic Negotiations, in D. Petcu et. al. (eds) Proceedings of SYNASC04: Symbolic and Numeric Algorithms for Scientific Computing, Mirton Press, Timisoara, Romania, pp. 369-380

Sycara,K.P. (1998). "Multiagent Systems," AI Magazine vol. 19(2), pp. 79-92

Sheng, Y.P. (2004) A dynamic adaptive bargaining algorithm for intelligent software agents in electronic commerce, International Journal of Computers, Systems and Signals, Vol. 5, No. 1, 2004

Takayuki, I., Hattori, H., and Klein, M. (2007). Multi-Issue Negotiation Protocol for Agents: Exploring Nonlinear Utility Spaces, IJCAI-07, pp1347-1352.

The Eclipse Platform, See http://www.eclipse.org/

Wooldridge M (2009) Introduction to Multiagent Systems, 2nd Edition, John Wiley and Sons, UK

Yoshikawa, S., Kamiryo, T., Yasumura, Y., & Uehara, K. (2006). Strategy Acquisition of Agents in Multi-Issue Negotiation. ACM International Conference of Web Intelligence

5

Adaptive Virtual Environments: The Role of Intelligent Agents

Marcus S. de Aquino[1] and Fernando da F. de Souza[2]
[1]*Federal University of Campina Grande,*
[2]*Federal University of Pernambuco,*
Brazil

1. Introduction

The aim of this chapter is to provide an understanding of how intelligent agents can improve user interaction to three-dimensional (3D) Virtual Environments by turning the later into an adaptive system.

A virtual environment (VE) can simulate a real environment or provide imaginary or even physically impossible scenarios. It allows one or more users to interact through visualization and manipulation of extremely complex representations (Frery, 2002). According to Chittaro & Ranon (2007), a VE can help people through direct experience by performing tasks that are suited to the learning or simulation tasks. Moreover, employing interactive 3D objects allows for more useful representations of subjects or sensations, offering the possibility of analyzing the same subject from different points of view. VE is defined here as a computer-generated, graphically-rich 3D world which the user can explore and perform actions on real time. The environment is based on 3D computer models and the user can navigate on the environment and interact with the 3D objects and other avatars existing there. The user's view of the environment is rendered dynamically and can be updated as the user moves.

More recently, three-dimensional Virtual Environments developed with Virtual Reality (VR) technologies and Graphical Computation techniques are emerging on the Web (Aquino et al., 2005, 2007, 2008). This makes it possible to build VEs more aware of their users. Moreover, it favors interactions with users bearing different profiles, cultures and knowledge levels. Under this paradigm, dynamic and interactive elements are introduced to VEs in order to increase their users' engagement. Such users' participations are directly related to both the environment and the feedback the system supplies him/her with. Accompaniment procedures to users' actions and updating VR environments accordingly have been used to accomplish this.

The personalization of VEs can enhance user's interaction in several applications such as distance-learning systems, to which students with different knowledge levels are remotely connected to interact with media, content and even to each other; electronic games for both amusement and learning; building construction providing different perspectives for architects, civil engineers, interior decorators and buyers; and to enable different kinds of access to specific systems e.g. a university information system that can be accessed by lecturers, students and other personnel. In this context, an adaptive VE shall be capable of managing the alterations that are occurring in the environment, to survey the user's behavior, to identify his/her eventual difficulties and, therefore, to suggest modifications in order to improve the user's interaction with the environment. Thus, VEs may take care of the user's necessities to guide his/her navigation in the environment. For instance, for those users that have previously interacted with the VE, the system may identify new ways of navigation or even reduce the number of steps needed for the interaction.

The need of user-aware 3D environments has contributed to the development of techniques to personalize VEs. One of such techniques has to do with using intelligent agents to identify user's actions and to adapt the environment according to the user's needs and his/her knowledge level. The use of intelligent entities (agents) and different forms of interactions makes it possible to build such environments, promoting bigger dynamism, realism and usability to them (Santos & Osório, 2004).

According to Russell & Norvig (2010), an agent has knowledge on the environment that it acts and on the actions that it can execute. The agent's behavior can be based on its own experience, as well as in the knowledge acquired from the particular environment it acts.

On the other hand, according to Celentano et al. (2004), an adaptive Virtual Environment must have intelligence to bring up to date the 3D environment with the objective to reduce the cognitive necessity of interaction. In such a way, the system can assist the user during the interaction by modifying the complexity of the environment or facilitating the navigation process.

Agents in decision-making processes allow constructing a more dynamic system in two main ways. Firstly, the choice of specific languages facilitates the capacity of communication between agents. Secondly, the determination of objectives, plans and actions makes it possible to model inference systems with enhanced precision.

The advantages of using agents are threefold: (i) to interact with the environment (and the user) through sensors and actuators; (ii) to evaluate the current state of the environment based on a knowledge base; and (iii) to make intelligent decisions in accordance with objectives to be reached (Russel & Norvig, 2010).

To achieve on-line VE updating, it must be guaranteed a communication protocol that keeps the connection of the active user and identifies his/her actions (plus underlying intentions) thoughtfully. Having this kind of information, an intelligent decision system must be activated to interpret such actions and to send a reply to the user accordingly. In adaptive VEs, the reply is translated into modifications to the environment, adapting the system to user's necessities (reduction/increasing the environment complexity level and access authorization, amongst others).

According to Woldrigde (2009), "there is obvious potential for marrying agent technology with that of computer games and virtual reality… In this case, the agents need to show emotions; to act and react in a way that resonates in tune with our empathy and understanding of human behavior".

2. Adaptive virtual environments

Adaptive VEs are addressed in this section, which highlights the techniques that may be employed to build such systems. These techniques are used for dynamic organization of objects on the environment (e.g., products more likely to interest the customer are shown in first plan in a virtual store) to facilitate the navigation and the exploration, in order to provide a more effective interaction. The adaptation can also modify the level of complexity of 3D objects according to the user´s knowledge degree on the environment. This aids VEs to deal more properly with their users' characteristics and necessities.

Some related works will be addressed below with the objective to illustrate several applications of intelligent agents in VE and to identify, in each case, the used techniques and the limitations on the generation of adaptive VEs.

The use of avatars as interactive guides in three-dimensional environments is proposed by Frery et al. (2002). The user's profile, obtained from forms (explicit collect) is identified and stored into the user model of the system's knowledge base. Having this information, the avatar (an intelligent agent) is capable to generate the strategy of navigation for the environment, as well as its graphical representation that will represent the user.

Even though only an explicit information collecting is carried out at the beginning of a session, there is already a concern with the identification of the user's characteristics and its use for adaptive environment construction.

However, although the environment is adaptable (the user's characteristics are used to generate the route for contents presentation), it is considered static because it does not make environment modification to adapt itself to the user's interests and necessities. In this case, the intelligent agent does not use its sensors to identify the user's interaction.

Chittaro & Ranon (2002a) developed the AWE3D (Adaptive WEb 3D), an adaptive VE that represents a virtual store in a Web environment, in which the users can browse and get information on objects spread over the environment. Information on the interests of the user, intended for the personalization of the environment, is obtained though explicit collect by monitoring user's actions in the environment (such as visualized products and effected purchases).

The environment is dynamic (possessing better interactivity with the user) and adaptable as well. Therefore, objects' presentation varies due to the customer's profile of purchase, which considers his/her necessities, preferences, visualization of products and options of purchase.

In this case, agents use their sensors to bring up to date the user's profile but they do not make the VE adaptation on real time, that is, they do not use its actuators to modify the VE with the objective, for example, to offer new promotion products (e.g., "loss leader").

In a posterior work, Chittaro et al. (2003) present a virtual agent assigned to assist the user to navigate on a virtual museum. From the description of the places or objects of interest to be visited, supplied at the beginning of a session, the agent creates an appropriate trajectory. Such an agent can also stop during its passage to present each object or place of interest previously determined by the user.

The trajectory is calculated by the Trajectory Manager whose task is to derive an appropriate sequence from the navigation points to pass by the objects that must be visualized by the user. The Trajectory Manager is inserted into the AWE3D environment to provide an additional resource to the adaptive environment.

The users' help system, carried out by an agent, is one of the strongest points of the work. It determines the route for presentation according to the users' interests. The environment is adaptable since it uses the user's profile to generate the trajectory. It is static because it does not modify the trajectory during a user's interaction with the virtual world.

The agent's sensors and actuators are used only to present the information asked by the user. The specific trajectory for the user's profile is defined at the beginning of a session and it does not provide adaptation on real time. Such an adaptation could be useful should the user be interested to see other objects of the museum that were not defined in the predefined route.

Santos & Osório (2004) has proposed the AdapTIVE environment (Adaptive Three-dimensional Intelligent and Virtual Environment) that shows adapted contents in accordance with both the interests of the users and the manipulation (insertion, removal or update) of contents on the environment.

A process of automatic categorization is applied to the creation of models of contents that are used in the spatial organization of the environment. The adaptation process uses models of both users and contents. Moreover, an intelligent virtual agent acts as assistant to the users with navigation and localization of relevant information.

The architecture of AdapTIVE presents an agent located in the customer's machine, which follows all the requests of the user in the virtual environment and guides him/her on searching for the desired information.

The agent in the AdapTIVE environment plays an important role on assisting navigation and to inform user's actions to the system, such as visited environments and accessed contents. Having such information, the system updates both the user model and the contents model in order to be able to reorganize the environment for a posterior session (defined by the system).

AdapTIVE is a static environment because it does not support object movements. However, it is an adaptable environment because it is concerned with adaptation of contents according to the user's profile.

In this case, the agent's sensors and actuators are used to guide users and to assist them on the VE. Its updating is carried out on posterior session rather than on real time. This kind of adaptation could contribute to present new contents to the user when he/she accesses a specific content.

An example of using multiagent system in VEs is ICSpace (Internet Culture Space) (Tavares et al., 2001). It has been proposed in order to support the interaction between different users visiting a same place. The agent based mechanisms will be responsible for taking the user into an interactive tour through a museum. They are able to show a same exposition personalized for each visitor. According to the places visited by the user, they can suggest either to see a particular work or to interact with other user with a similar profile (Tavares et al., 2005).

The agents' architecture structure is composed of three layers. The reactive layer has as its goal to perceive user actions on the environment. The intermediate layer is responsible for maintaining the knowledge database using a Database Agent to do this work. Finally, the service layer is capable of processing information and provides services to users.

The functionalities offered by service agents are: to build the user profile; to organize the exhibition according to the user's profile; to recommend service in accordance with the audience of works and rooms; to guide visitors in the environment rooms; and to encourage interpersonal communication between users through the use of communication tools.

Different agents' categories have been defined in the work. Each one of them identifies a specific role in the multiagent system architecture with a special function in a cultural environment context.

Thus, it can be seen that the layered division of the agents' tasks allows better accompaniment of the users' actions and a greater capacity in the decision making process. In this case, objects do not suffer modification on the VE (it is a static one), but the route suggested to the user becomes adaptable according with his/her profile. However, agents do not update the VE on real time. This could be useful should the user acquire new knowledge from the objects visited in the museum.

Costa et al. (2010) present a proposal to control the user's navigation on 3D games using intelligent agents. An application of their work was developed aimed at training the memory concentration capacity for patients with attention deficit.

They explore the integration of multiagent model methodologies to control the user performance, adapting the interface and automatically changing the difficulty level of tasks.

To support every phase of modeling and implementation of agents, a lexical catalog was specified to record and document the requirements. They defined four agents that are responsible for planning patient care; controlling the interactions to the game; analyzing the performance of the patient; and setting up the environment. It was defined twenty agents' behaviors that were implemented in the JADE framework (Bellifemine, 2003).

A system application proposes a scene which depicts bookshelves with different objects on them. Objects are randomly shown on a table and the patient must walk to one shelf and choose a similar one. Agents will monitor the time and the user interactions with the environment. They will control the rights and wrongs answers and combine these data with the information about the patient's impairments. The therapist informs the patient personal data when registering him/her in the system.

The advantage of their work is that the accompaniment of the patient's activities is managed by the agents. Moreover, they are capable to consider new activities with different levels of difficulties, depending on the correctness/incorrectness of the patient's attempt.

So, the multiagent system works to submit a problem to the user, to evaluate his/her actions and, after that, to generate new situations with different levels of difficulty. Agents work in group to reach an objective and, therefore, they increase the capacity of the system to interact with the user and to generate a suitable environment to the user model.

Cai et al. (2011) propose to simulate a coalmine risk accidents using virtual reality and multiagent technology. Agents are grouped into either Entity Agents or Service Agents.

Entity Agents endow the geometric entities rendered in bottom layer with specific semantics and behavior rules. Service Agents are responsible to support the network communication; to provide semantic information service related to the virtual environment, and primarily offer the necessary knowledge for intelligent behaviors of a coalmine virtual environment; and to provide services related to specific applications.

Risk accidents in coalmine are simulated by agents. On the course of moving though the panned paths, the virtual miner may encounter some obstacles or hazards such as unsupported roof, uncovered holes, uneven surfaces, or electrical cables. Virtual miner's tiredness value also will increase as fulfillment of safety inspection tasks. In this case, driven by its desire of going out of the underground mine, the virtual miner neglected an approaching locomotive and hurried to go through a crosscut. As a result, the virtual miner was seriously injured. Therefore, this approach can reconstruct risk accidents to enable better understanding risk factors in emergency situation and to assist interactive risk analysis in underground coalmine as well.

It is noticed that the division of tasks in a Multiagent System (MAS) can be very useful in a simulation environment. It is possible to generate several dangerous situations and to verify the behavior that would be carried through by a user (in this case, the behavior of the user is controlled by an avatar/intelligent agent). Although in this application it is not necessary the adaptation on real time, the MAS can generate several suitable scenes to the possible risk situations that can be found in a coalmine.

As it can be seen in the above examples, agents are capable to generate applications in accordance with the preferences and interests of the system's users. However, this requires the inclusion of new techniques to construct VEs nearest to the reality.

User's modeling techniques, for example, have been incorporated to these applications with the objective to identify the user's characteristics, necessities and preferences. According to Papatheodorou (2001), one of the key benefits of building systems capable of modeling the user is the possibility of adapting the system behavior to particular needs of their users.

A user model (UM) is a representation of the user properties, which allows the system to adapt aspects of its performance and its functionalities to individual necessities. To reach this objective, modeling techniques have been developed from the user's profile identification. Besides the conventional characteristics of the user, others can effectively be added to the model in order to describe the carried out actions (selected objects and contents accesses) as well as how the interaction is made (preferences for the environment organization, forms of navigation, type of preferred interface and knowledge acquired during the interaction with the environment).

The works of Chittaro & Ranon (2000a, 2000b, 2002a, 2002b) propose the adoption of a user template for customizing a 3D environment. Their proposal is aimed at deploying a user template to adjust the layout structure of a Web store. Besides, the adaptive VE AWE3D (Chittaro & Ranon, 2000a) is a pioneer in the literature on using UM to provide adaptation for a three-dimensional environment. The use of a form and the association of a user to a pre-defined profile contribute to the customization of a 3D environment.

Santos & Osório (2004) also deploys user template to generate a virtual adaptive environment. Their proposal obtains user profile information through a data collection form for composition of the initial model. As the user interacts with the environment, evidences of navigation, and request access to contents are collected and used in the process of updating the user template. Even though, the UM is updated during the session, the use of this information for the environment transformation can only be done offline. Tavares et al. (2005) use the UM: i) to suggest to the current user to see a particular work; and ii) to interact with another user bearing a similar profile. Costa et al. (2010) also use UM to control users' navigation on 3D games taking into consideration their profiles.

Table 1 summarizes the analysis carried out on the focused environments. It was based on i) the type of environment; ii) whether it uses agents or not; iii) the kind of agent-user interaction; iv) how the user's profile is dealt with by the system; and v) whether it is adaptive or not. The characteristics of agents and environments considered in the analysis are based on those presented by Russel & Norvig (2010).

It is also verified, in Table 1, that the systems that possess the module User Profile, and carry out explicit and/or implicit collection, use such information either to modify the environment or just to provide a guided navigation to the user. Thus, the works of Chittaro & Ranon (2002a), Santos & Osório (2004), Costa et al. (2010) and Cai et al. (2011) are those that perform scenes alterations. The works of Frery et al. (206.02), Chittaro et al. (2003) and Tavares et al. (2005) modify user´s routes with no alterations to the environment. However, none of them allows alterations due to modifications on the user profile to occur on real time.

The use of Artificial Intelligence in virtual environments made it possible the construction of virtual worlds closer to the user's reality. The deployment of intelligent agents in such environments allows, for example, the presence of assistants to help with the navigation or to act as a communication interface whenever the user needs to get some information or explanation on determined subject.

The inclusion of the user's profile in VEs enables the generation of personalized environments. The latter are capable of adapting their contents according to the user's preferences, his/her navigation style and cognitive capacity. Thus, a personalized environment may increase the satisfaction and productivity of its users.

One of the limitations found on current adaptive VE is the lack of real time (on-line) evolution, which would allow updating a virtual world during the user's interaction. Such a property may enhance to a large extent the range of applications that can be supported by such environments, mainly those that cannot wait for the next user's interaction to benefit from the system updating.

Objects manipulation on real time occurs when the system detects some user's action that implies scene changing. This change may need modifying one or more scene objects, but not necessarily the reloading of the whole environment. VEs focused above perform their modifications off-line and introduce them only in the next user's interaction.

An adaptive VE must identify each user's profile at the beginning of a session to be able to determine the most adequate environment to be generated. Thus, the representation of the virtual world must allow 3D objects to be inserted to or removed from the environment in order to provide such tailored updates. Furthermore, such updating should be carried out on real time.

System	Type of Environment	Agent / User Interaction	User Profile	Adaptive environ-ment	Real Time Adaptivity
Frery et al. (2002)	3D/2D, entertainment, static	Aid to navigation and suggestions making	Explicit collection (form), individual, static	No	No
Chittaro & Ranon (2002a)	3D, *e-commerce*, dynamic	Consultation, aid to navigation	Explicit and implicit collections, individual and group, dynamic	Yes	No
Chittaro et al. (2003)	3D, entertainment, static	Aid to navigation	Explicit collection (forms), individual, static	No	No
Santos & Osório (2004)	3D/2D, contents presentation, static	Consultation, aid to navigation	Explicit and implicit collections, individual, static	Yes	No
Tavares et al. (2005)	3D/2D, entertainment, static	Aid to navigation and suggestions making, aid to communication	Implicit and explicit collections, individual and group, static	No	No
Costa et al. (2010)	3D, serious game, dynamic	User's actions evaluation	Implicit and explicit collections, individual, static	Yes	No
Cai et al. (2011)	3D, simulation, static	It does not have (the agent simulates the user)	Implicit and explicit collections, individual, static	Yes	No

Table 1. A Comparative Analysis between Adaptive VEs

Bearing in mind the above considerations, we present VEPersonal (Aquino et al., 2010) as a solution to the problem of VE content real time adaptation by using a Multiagent System (MAS) capable of handling virtual objects with different complexity levels. VEPersonal is responsible for the creation and maintenance of adaptive three-dimensional environments in the Web. It is also capable of modifying the world according to the user's cognitive evolution. The system chooses the proper level of detail to display according to the user's needs, knowledge and characteristics detected from his/her profile. Moreover, VEPersonal makes it possible a real time adaptation through the insertion and removal of objects into/from the scene according to the users' actions.

3. Agents and adaptive systems

Multiagent Systems are characterized for the existence of more than one agent which may interact between them independently as well as they may work in group to execute tasks, to solve problems or to meet a particular objective. Such objectives can be common to all agents or not (Lesser, 1999). Each agent can communicate or cooperate with other agents when necessary, with the objective to add the local results to reach the solution of the general problem (Jennings, 2000). To meet an objective, it is necessary to define good mechanisms of communication (exchange of messages), cooperation (assistance) and coordination (organization) in the multiagent system. Different agents may have different "spheres of influence". These spheres of influence may coincide in some cases. Then, it may give rise to dependence relationships between agents (Woldridge, 2009). Therefore, an agent can cooperate with other agents that have influence on other environments.

According to Ferber (1999), a MAS is applied to a system comprising the following elements: an environment; a set of objects that can be perceived, created, destroyed and modified by agents; an assembly of agents which represent the active entities of the system; an assembly of relations, which link objects to each other; an assembly of operations to make it possible for the agents to perceive, produce, consume, transform and manipulate objects; and operators with the task of representing the application of such operations and the reaction of the world to this modification attempt.

3.1 The society of agents in VEPersonal

In the Virtual Environment we will be able to have an organization of responsible agents for a system of roles in different dimensions (interface and monitoring user's actions, decision-making, storage and management of information and modifications in the VE for example).

To satisfy these necessities, we developed the VEPersonal architecture, shown in Figure 1. The characteristics of the users plus their behaviors are stored into the User Model (UM) as well as the history of the environment changes into the Environment Model (EM). Such information is obtained from the interface through sensors that detect the actions undertaken by the user. Thus, the system can monitor progress during a user's interaction and can create or modify objects on the underlying virtual world accordingly.

Data structures in VEPersonal are stored into a Data Base Management System (DBMS) in order to guarantee a higher data integrity and integration. User's personal data records and the environment information are stored using a DBMS relational structure. 3D objects use a

XML structure because they are constructed using the X3D language (X3D, 2007). Data recovery and in-memory management are performed by the agents society. Each agent is responsible for manipulating just one type of information. Moreover, information exchanging must comply with a specific ontology, and it is coordinated by a master agent. Therefore, both communication and information analysis are more consistent.

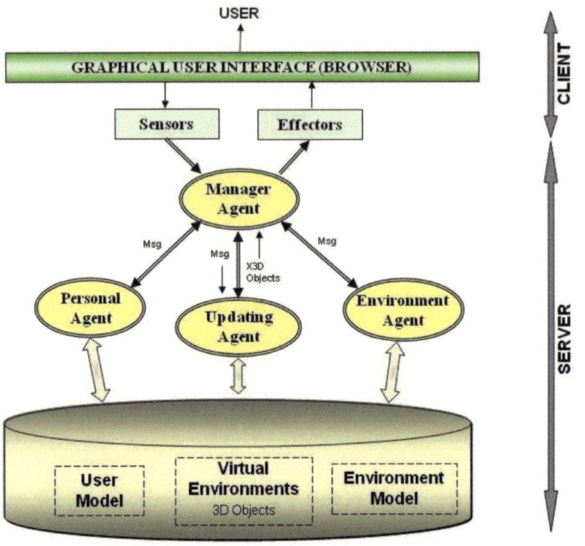

Fig. 1. The VEPersonal architecture

An important concept to be considered is levels of organization. It allows embedding one level into another. Therefore, it is appropriate to consider an organization as an aggregation of elements from a lower level as well as a component of the organization for a higher level (Ferber, 1999). Thus, in VEPersonal, the tasks were distributed according to the necessities to manage the environment and to generate the adaptations. It was defined which agents to do what, which resources should be used, and chosen goals and skills.

Four agents compose the society of agents (Aquino et al., 2007). The Manager Agent is responsible for monitoring the user's actions as well as the current state of the virtual environment. It also determines the tasks to be carried out by other agents and coordinates communication between them. The Personal Agent determines the user's profile and updates the UM whenever any change to the profile is detected. It has an inference system in its knowledge base that evaluates user's knowledge. The Environment Agent verifies the current state of the virtual environment and stores the changes into the EM. The Updating Agent is responsible for updating the virtual world based on the information provided by other agents.

During the decision-making process, the Manager Agent consults the Environment Agent about the current structure of the VE (stored in the EM). It also consults the Personal Agent to identify the user's profile (stored in UM). This information is sent to the Updating Agent, which generates queries to a database to recover objects to be used for updating the virtual world. Next, the recovered objects are sent to the Manager Agent that generates the 3D structure of the virtual environment and sends it to the user interface. Following, the architecture of each agent with its respective functions is described.

3.1.1 Manager Agent

The Manager Agent is responsible for coordinating the other agents' actions: it gets the user's actions from the interface, it identifies the type of action to be performed, and it dispatches the action to the responsible agent. It also has methods to initiate the behaviors of others agents. Each behavior generates a message that includes the agent sender, the agent receiver, the message's content and the action to be carried through. The internal architecture of the Manager Agent is shown in Figure 2.

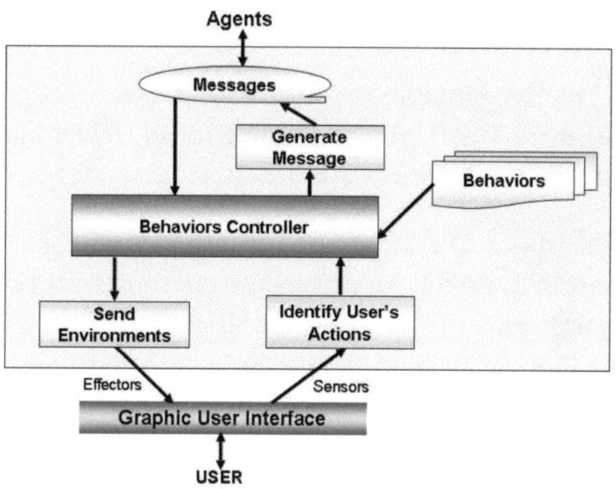

Fig. 2. Manager Agent architecture

The main component of the architecture is the Behavior Controller. It is used to supervise the requests sent to agents and verifies if the solicitations have been attended. The requests are carried out by message exchanging between agents. Its behavior is defined by a set of rules stored on its behaviors base.

3.1.2 Personal Agent

When the user accesses VEPersonal for the first time, an initial form is presented to him/her. Then, the user supplies information about points of interests, knowledge's level and needs. After the fulfillment of the form, the Personal Agent determines the initial user's profile. The form and the profile are stored in the UM. The determination of the profile and its updating is made by inference rules stored on the Profile Controller (Figure 3).

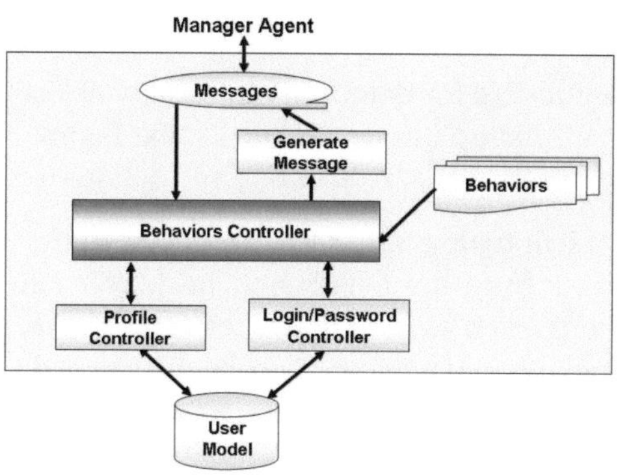

Fig. 3. Personal Agent architecture

The Personal Agent is a reactive agent. Therefore, it is only activated under a demand by the Manager Agent. The Personal Agent uses a logic-based system of inference that takes into account the user information that is held by the system. This technique is appropriate for reactive agents because the knowledge base of rules is activated due to the perception of the environment, and reacts through an action (for example, to store a specific information on the UM). The Personal Agent is responsible for supplying the user profile whenever the Manager Agent requests so.

3.1.3 Environment Agent

The Environment Agent is responsible for verifying the occurred modifications in the environment and for updating the Environment Model. This agent is also reactive. It is activated only when the Manager Agent demands it.

The Environment Model is updated whenever the Updating Agent generates a new virtual world or it defines new objects to be inserted into the current environment. This information is sent to the Manager Agent and dispatched to the Environment Agent that stores the modifications on the EM (Figure 4). The Environment Agent provides current information about objects of the environment (stored on the EM) whenever the Manager Agent requests it.

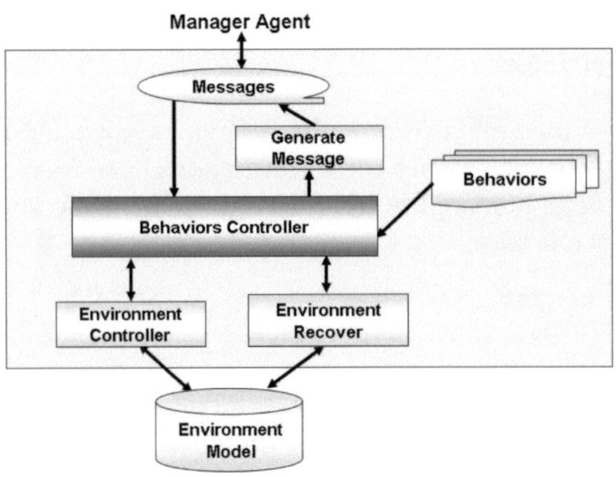

Fig. 4. Environment Agent architecture

3.1.4 Updating Agent

The Updating Agent is responsible for determining the new objects to be requested from the DBMS and added to the VE for updating the world (see Figure 5). It is a cognitive agent because it has objectives to reach, plans to elaborate and actions to perform.

Amongst its objectives is the updating of the VEs according to the user needs. Plans must be elaborated to request objects from the DBMS and to deliver new objects to the Manager Agent. A sequence of actions, such as identifying the user profile, generating queries to the DBMS and communicating with other agents must be determined.

The Updating Agent uses its knowledge base to evaluate the current state of the environment and, according to the objectives to be reached, it determines the necessary modifications to adapt the system to the user's profile.

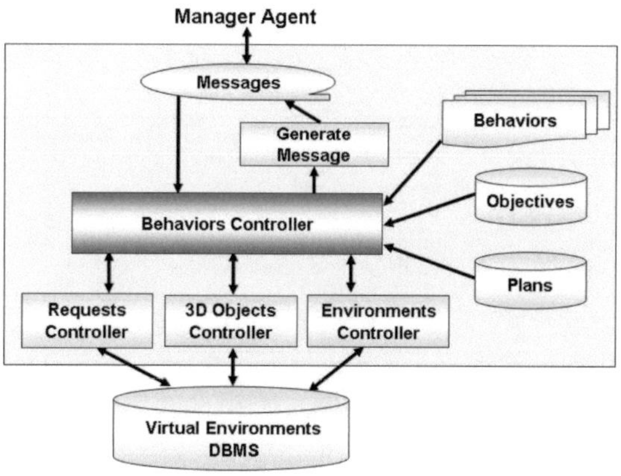

Fig. 5. Updating Agent architecture

3.2 The Agents' communication

Communication between agents is accomplished by using JADE (Java Agent Development framework, 2011), an application based on agents according to the Foundation for Intelligent Physical Agents specifications (FIPA, 2011). Message exchanging between agents is governed by a set of communication terms indicating the intent of the sender (the agent) to send a message. This communication promotes the necessary information retrieval that will allow updating the environment. Examples of communication terms defined by FIPA are: REQUEST - the issuer is requesting for some action to be performed; INFORM - the issuer is informing the result of some action; QUERY - the issuer is asking for recovering the reference to some object.

Agents' behavior is obtained considering the following features: user registration; a new environment request; an already visited environment request; a profile change assessment; and to determine possible changes to the user's profile. Each of these features is triggered by the Manager Agent, since it controls the actions of other agents on the system (Aquino & Souza, 2010). Due to the above, knowledge can be seen as a result of interactions between cognitive agents. Concepts, theories and laws, thus, can come out from a process of confrontation, objections, proof and refutations (Ferber, 1999).

Both confrontations with the world and communications with other agents are equally present under the concept of "interaction". Thus, specific learning that comes from confrontations between individuals and the world allied to the know-how that comes from interactions one individual can have with other individuals is another way to define knowledge (Ferber, 1999). As an example, Figure 6 describes the case where the user requests an environment that he/she has not yet visited (the system store all users' visited environments in the EM).

The interface sends the request to the Manager Agent. The later, initially, asks the Personal Agent for the user profile via a message (Msg 1. QUERY-REF). This agent queries a database to retrieve the user's knowledge level on the environment (userLevel) assigned to the current user, e.g. "beginner". When receiving the user profile from the Personal Agent (Msg 2. INFORM_REF), the Manager Agent asks the Environment Agent whether the user has already visited the requested environment.

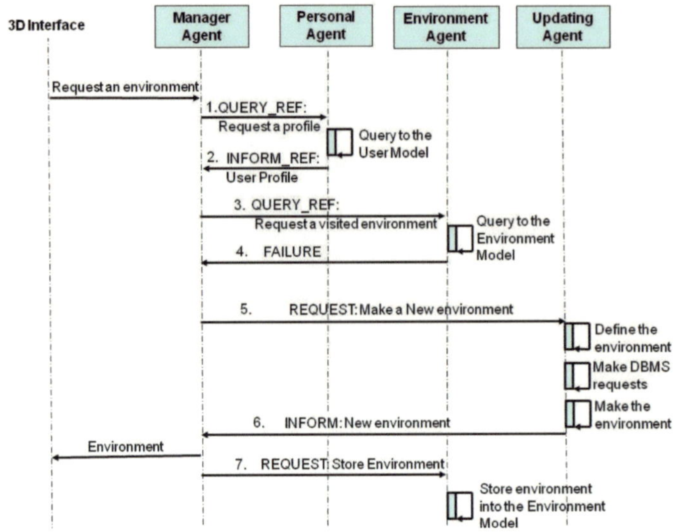

Fig. 6. Request for a new environment

The Environment Agent queries the Environment Model to learn if there is an association of any environment to the user (Msg. 3. QUERY_REF). Since it is a request for a new environment, the answer is empty, indicating that the user has not yet visited that environment (Msg 4. FAILURE). Each environment deals with a particular knowledge domain e.g. experiments on Physics.

Having the answer, the Manager Agent sends a message to the Updating Agent requesting a new environment (Msg 5. REQUEST), for example, a Free Fall experiment from the Physics domain. This agent performs the following steps: Environment definition - queries the database to find out the identity of the environment to be retrieved and objects that belong to such an environment; Database queries generation - retrieves the X3D code of objects belonging to the environment; and Environment Generation - to build the environment with the X3D codes of objects, inserting the X3D file header.

Next, a message from the Updating Agent is sent to the Manager Agent to inform that the operation has succeeded (Msg 6.INFORM_REF), and the X3D code for the created environment is appended. The Manager Agent sends the environment to the Web interface that, for its turn, sends it to the user's browser. The former sends also a message (Msg 7.REQUEST) having the objects that compose the environment to the Environment Agent, which stores such data into the Environment Model.

Once the message with the user profile changing received, the Manager Agent sends through the interface, a message to the user stating that there was a change from his/her profile and that the environment will be updated. It is given the option to accept the change or not. This procedure is performed in order that the user may be aware that changes will occur in the environment.

If such a user accepts that (see Figure 7), the Manager Agent asks the Environment Agent for the current environment that the user is interacting with (Msg 1. QUERY_REF). The Environment Agent queries the Environment Model; it retrieves the list of objects belonging to the current environment; and sends it to the Manager Agent (Msg 2. INFORM_REF). This agent writes a message to the Updating Agent to request the generation of the environment with the new profile (Msg 3. REQUEST).

The role of the Updating Agent now is to search into a database the list of objects that have the new profile defined for the user e.g. "intermediary". The objects found for this profile are retrieved. A message to return the list of names of objects with their X3D codes is then sent to the Manager Agent (Msg 4. INFORM_REF). Next, the Manager Agent sends that list to the interface.

The purpose of this list of objects (names plus X3D code) is to allow the interface to perform only the replacement for objects that need to be modified in the environment. Thus, it is not necessary to reload the entire VE due to the profile changing, which reduces the overhead in the process of data transmission while avoiding the scene rebooting as well.

The updating of the environment is also informed to the Environment Agent (Msg 5. REQUEST). A list with the names of the objects is sent to this agent that will update the Environment Model accordingly.

VEPersonal uses a Web environment for communicating with the user who is connected remotely. An interface for communication between the user and the system has been developed to achieve the synchronization of information in order to be a dynamic environment. Due to the amount of information that must be stored, retrieved and processed in a VE, a client-server application becomes more appropriate, decreasing the burden on the client machine. All the communication process will be detailed on the following subsection.

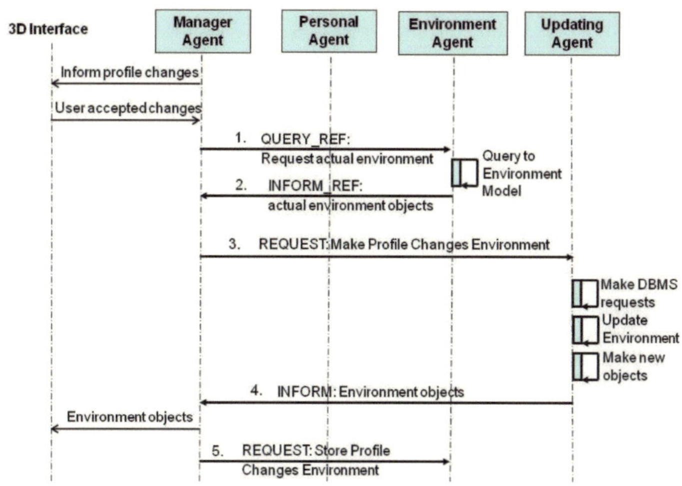

Fig. 7. Generation of a new VE depending on Profile Changing

3.3 Client-server communication

The interface task is to communicate the actions performed by the user to the Manager Agent, in addition to receiving objects to update the virtual world. This updating can be by sending a complete X3D environment, insertion of new objects (tags X3D) or removal of objects (by name) that exist in the VE. The interface should dispose means to aid the Manager Agent to carry out such operations.

The Xj3D browser (Xj3D, 2007) performs the visualization of virtual worlds. This browser is an open source project of the Web3D Consortium (Web3D, 2007), developed in Java, which allows viewing X3D and VRML environments. Applications using Xj3D have been developed for simulation, training and education as well as for medical visualization, games and projects involving viewing sensors (Matsuba, 2007). Besides that browser, the API Scene Access Interface (SAI, 2007) was used to establish communication between X3D environments and Java. This API allows for the insertion, deletion and modification of the objects in the Xj3D browser in real time.

The integration of these features in the Web environment used the Java Web Start technology (JWS, 2007) in order to enable the execution of Web applications, managing services and communications protocols. JWS is initiated automatically when it is done the first download of the VEPersonal application. JWS stores the application locally, thus, all the subsequent initiations are nearly instantaneous, since all of the needed resources are already available.

On the client side, the user accesses the system via the browser and can perform actions such as registration and authentication. When he/she requests the generation of the 3D world, a Java application is initiated to monitor the user actions in the environment and to inform to the server about the execution of an action (e.g. click of the mouse or proximity to objects). This application is also responsible for receiving the virtual world to be loaded or objects to be included and/or excluded in/from such a world (Figure 8).

On the server side, when an action is received from the user, the Manager Agent is responsible for determining what should be the actions to be performed. These actions are transformed into messages from the protocol and sent to the other agents. The society of agents takes the necessary decisions and returns to the interface the corresponding updating of the virtual world, if necessary.

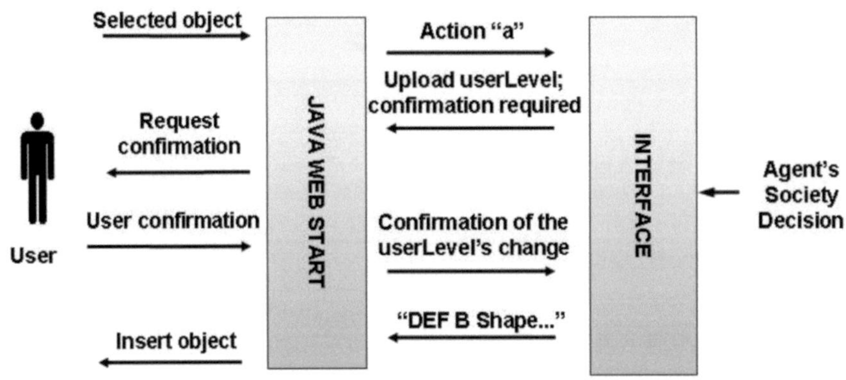

Fig. 8. Client-server interface of VEPersonal using Java Web Start

The communication interface of VEPersonal was structured in a way that the client-server connection could be performed decoupled. Figure 9 presents the structure of the interface and the project's design patterns used in the communication between the client and the server.

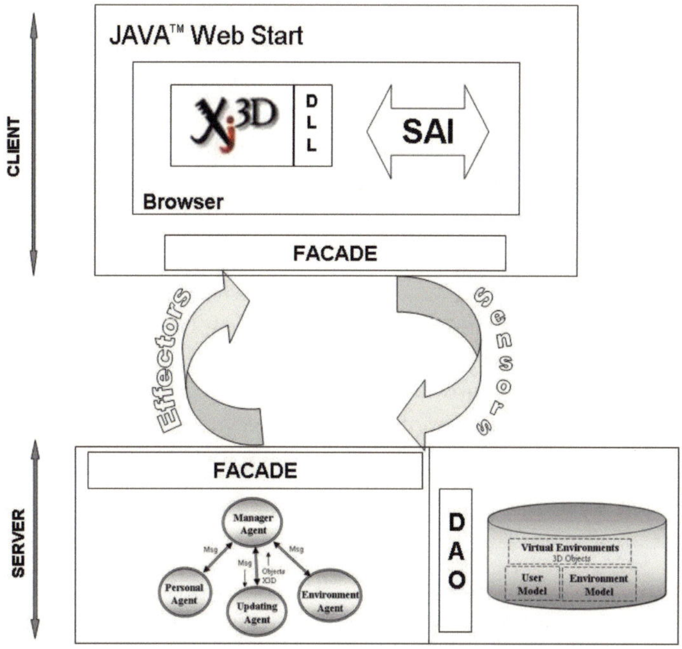

Fig. 9. The VEPersonal's interface structure and the used design patterns

On the client machine, the execution of the Xj3D browser needs various dynamic-link libraries (DLL, 2007). To make the application decoupled, that is, independent of the location of the library, it was built a Load function that locates and loads automatically to the client's machine the required libraries to the application. In this case, the application can run on any machine because it does not depend on external libraries.

The Interface in VEPersonal is responsible for communicating the application (which is running in the browser) with the server. This communication occurs through sensors and effectors. The sensors notify the changes made on the browser, identifying the object and the type of action performed by the user. For the implementation of the sensors it has been defined a method (Listener), which uses the design pattern Observer. This pattern defines a dependence on one-to-many between objects, so that when an object changes its state, all their dependents are automatically notified and updated. In this case, the Listener is used to propagate to the server the changes occurring in the browser.

Effectors are responsible for sending objects and virtual environments from the server to the browser. Both effectors and sensors use the framework LipeRMI (LipeRMI, 2007) for data transfer between the client and server via Web.

LipeRMI re-implements a Remote Method Invocation (RMI, 2007) so that the calls are made over the Internet, minimizing the use of bandwidth for communication (reducing the number of active connections). Once the client is already connected, this connection should remain open throughout the session for data exchanging between client and server (or until the application allows the connection to be closed). Hence the server will never need to open a connection from server to client, since it may use the existing connection. Therefore, the client is not concerned with firewall control - solving the biggest RMI problem.

By using LipeRMI, communication is defined by events that activate the connections of the client and the server, checking when a connection is initiated and terminated. The main events performed by the client during communication with the interface are: to create a connection when the user logs on; to send messages to the server to inform users actions; and to get messages sent by the server. The server on its turn shall wait for a client message and, therefore, remains on waiting state performing the listening event. Once established a connection with the client, the server performs a sending or receiving event.

In order to abstract features of the browser and to decrease the coupling with the server, making the communication independent of the employed technology, the *Facade* design pattern was adapted. *Facade* is a structural pattern that aims at hiding the details of a process by creating a *Facade* class. The client, then, just calls a method of *Facade* class and this class is responsible for executing this process. A *Facade* was also developed for the server, specifying the patterns of communication with the interface.

The methods used by the interface to the *Facade* standard are: openEnvironment, setEnvironment, get ObjectList, addObject, removeObject, getX3dEnvironment, setUser-Profile, addVEPersonalEventListener, removeVEpersonalEventListener, exitEnvironment.

The Interface of VEPersonal performs client-server communication with high cohesion and low coupling due to the design patterns used. Such a police clearly allows the alteration or substitution of the employed technologies, whenever occur the launching of new technologies or evolution of the already existing.

4. Adaptivity in virtual environments – An example

We present in this section an example to illustrate the benefits that adaptivity can bring to VEs. Particularly, our solution can be used in environments with different levels of complexity for any given situation, which adds more flexibility to such systems. Thus, let´s consider a VE designed to teach Physics. It can present an experiment with different levels of questions regarding the student's knowledge. On the other hand, the system can allow the user to access a new environment (a room with other experiments) or new details if his/her profile is suitable for that.

Figure 10 shows the student interaction with a Free Fall experiment. The objective of the experiment is to study the acceleration of gravity. For each experiment the student can consult the underlying theory and perform further interactions. At this time, new objects are recovered from a database to be inserted into the virtual environment. The objects are defined in X3D language that is appropriate to construct VEs in the Web, as mentioned before.

For example, the object "evaluation test" is presented according to the interactions carried out by the user. This test is specific to the knowledge level of the student (according to his/her profile). The test for a beginner student, presented in Figure 10, is composed of a question and three answer options.

The test insertion into the environment is determined by VEPersonal's agents that receive information on student's actions, e.g. the number of executions of the experiment and the consulted theory. Rules to determine what to modify and when this must occur are inserted into the knowledge base of the Update Agent. This agent recovers X3D objects from the DBMS using information supplied by both the Personal and the Environment agents.

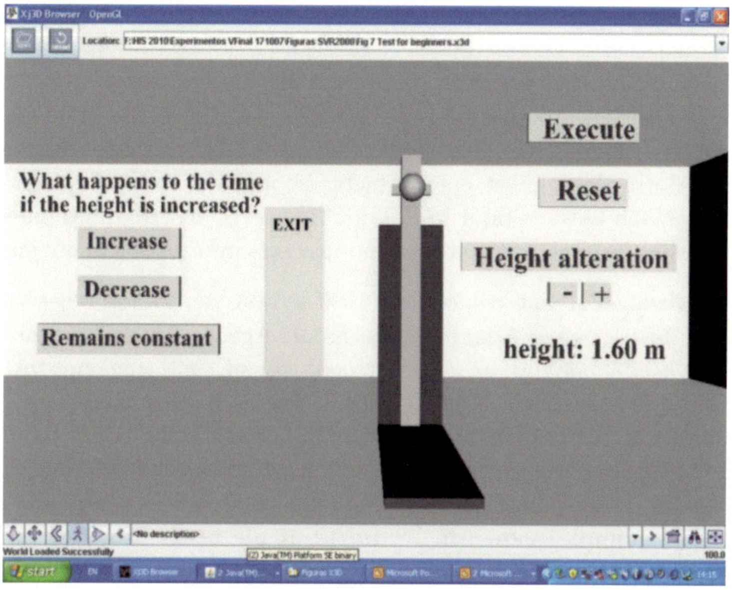

Fig. 10. Test for beginners

In the case of an experienced student (this information is provided by the Personal Agent through consultation to the user model of the student), a more elaborated question (with bigger rank of difficulty) is presented (Figure 11). Such a question is another object that replaces the beginners' question one. This object is also determined by the Update Agent.

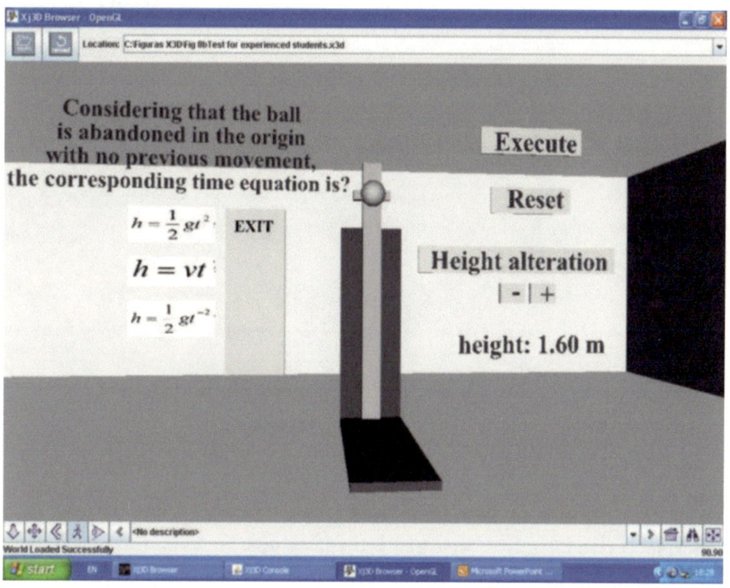

Fig. 11. Test for experienced students

Another advantage for constructing VEs with objects that are retrieved from a database is the possibility to determine the user's access priority. For example, the access to a room that has experiments on a given concept will only be granted to students that reached an adequate level of knowledge.

The Personal Agent is always bringing up to date the student's profile according with the number of right answers, number of experiments' executions, the kind of consultations carried out, amongst others. Thus, this agent is capable of determining whether the user has specific access priority to a given environment. Should the student possess appropriate knowledge for Newton Laws, a door to the right would be inserted into the virtual world. This permits the student to enter next room and to access information about such laws.

In this case, the Manager Agent, responsible for insertion/removal of objects, requests new objects to update the user's VE. After that, the Update Agent receives information from both the user's User Model, envoy by the Personal Agent, and the current state of the environment, envoy by the Environment Agent. Using such information, the Update Agent identifies the user's access priority and recovers the object "door" from the database. This object is envoy to the Manager Agent that inserts it into the user's VE. This modification in the environment is made immediately, without the necessity to reload the entire virtual environment. This example, shown in Figure 12, is the result of a real time adaptation according with modifications on the user's profile characteristics.

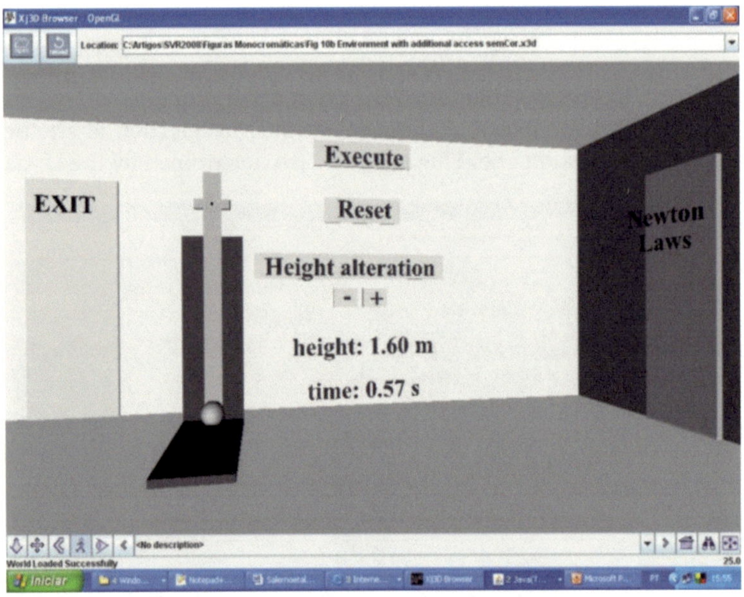

Fig. 12. Environment seen by user with additional access

5. Conclusions

This chapter discussed the benefits brought by adaptivity to VEs. Particularly, it has focused on the role played by agents on this context. Thus, we presented a way to build adaptive VE systems by using a society of agents. Two important points must be considered in order to increase the capacity of adaptive VEs: (i) to record properly the current state of the virtual environment; and (ii) to keep track of the modifications carried out by their users. These allow keeping the virtual environment up to date on both situations: during the current user interaction as well as on the next ones. All needed data are modeled into both a User Model (UM) responsible for all user characteristics, and an Environment Model that has to do with all properties of the virtual worlds.

In order to carry out the tasks described above it is necessary a quick and efficient decision making process allied to a precise implementation of the reached decisions. By automating the whole process, agents play the most important role to construct VEs that can adapt to their users' needs on real time.

A large number of applications exploit the User Model in order to adjust themselves to the necessities of the user or to propose changes that are of his/her interest. In 3D environments, particularly in adaptive VEs, the UM is a very important element, since it also stores the behavior of the user; his/her style of navigation; forms of interaction with the environment; and the evolution of the user's learning in the system. Thus, agents will be able to carry out the decision-making process for generating virtual worlds and eventual adaptations using the information contained in the UM.

The main concern with the representation of the UM in a virtual environment must be guided by the identification of the objects that the user can manipulate (to visualize, to approach and to select; existing different levels of perception for each case). It is also necessary to consider his/her interest for determined contents; his/her capacity of interaction; and, mainly, his/her evolution during the learning process. To achieve this, it is needed to construct a framework that may store specific user information (level of knowledge and manipulated objects, for instance) and of a model based on logic that interprets the necessary information to be represented in the UM taking into consideration the objectives and beliefs of the user.

The use of intelligent agents in VEs has the objective to increase the capacity of analysis of the environment by the distribution of tasks and by the incorporation of user modeling techniques on its knowledge base. In this context, intelligent agents contribute to increase the capacity of monitoring the user's actions and the identification of his/her profile. Consequently, the construction of an adaptive VE more precise and more dynamic can be carried out with better accuracy, due to the capacity of agents in interpreting the "intentions" of the user.

6. References

Aquino, M. S. & Souza, F. F. (2010). An intelligent web interface to generate and update adaptive virtual environments. *Proceedings of 10th International Conference on Hybrid Intelligent Systems*, v. 01. pp. 51-54, Atlanta, Georgia, USA, August 2010.

Aquino, M. S.; Souza, F. F.; Frery, A. C.; Souza, D. A. C. M.; Fujioka, R. C. & Vieira, M. M. S. (2008). An Infrastructure to Generate Adaptive Virtual Environments with the Management of Client-Server Communication in Real Time. *Proceedings of X*

Symposium on Virtual and Augmented Reality, Porto Alegre: Sociedade Brasileira de Computação, pp. 61-69, João Pessoa, Paraíba, Brazil, Mai 2008.

Aquino, M. S.; Souza, F. F.; Frery, A. C; Souza, D. A. C. M. & Fujioka, R. C. (2007). Supporting Adaptive Virtual Environments with Intelligent Agents. *Proceedings of 7th International Conference on Intelligent Systems Design and Applications - ISDA'07*, pp. 217-222, Rio de Janeiro-RJ, Brazil, October 2007.

Aquino, M. S.; Souza, F. F. & Frery, A. C. (2005). VEPersonal - An Infrastructure of Virtual Reality Components to Generate Web Adaptive Environments. In: Simpósio Brasileiro de Sistemas Multimídia e Web, WebMedia 2005, Poços de Caldas-MG, Brazil, *ACM International Conference Proceeding Series*, pp. 1-8, New York, USA: ACM Press, v. 125.

Bellifemine, F.; Caire, G.; Poggi, A. & Rimassa, G. (2003). *Java Agent DEvelopment Framework - JADE - A White Paper*. In: Telecom Italia EXP magazine, Volume 3, n. 3, September 2003. Available: http://jade.tilab.com/papers/2003/WhitePaperJADEEXP.pdf

Cai , L.; Zheng, X.; Qu, H. & Luo, Z. (2011). Risk Accident Simulation Using Virtual Reality and Multi-agent Technology. *JDCTA: International Journal of Digital Content Technology and its Applications*. Vol. 5, No. 2, (February, 2011) pp. 181-190, ISSN: 2233-9310 (Online), ISSN: 1975-9339 (Print).

Celentano, A.; Nodari, M. & Pittarello, F. (2004). Adaptive Interaction in Web3D Virtual Worlds. *Proceedings of Web3D 2004 - 9th International Conference on 3DWeb Technology*: ACM Press, ISBN:1-58113-845-8, pp. 41–50, Monterey, California, USA.

Chittaro L. & Ranon R. (2007). Adaptive Hypermedia Techniques for 3D Educational Virtual Environments. IEEE Intelligent Systems, Vol. 22, No. 4, (July-August 2004), pp. 31-37, ISSN: 1541-1672.

Chittaro, R.; Ranon, R. & Ieronutti, L. (2003). Guiding Visitors of Web3D Worlds through Automatically Generated Tours. Proceedings of Web3D 2003: 8th International Conference on 3D Web Technology, ACM Press, New York, pp. 27-38.

Chittaro, L. & Ranon, R. (2002a). New Directions for the Design of Virtual Reality Interfaces to E-Commerce Sites. *Proceedings of AVI 2002: 5th International Conference on Advanced Visual Interfaces*, ACM Press, New York, pp. 308-315.

Chittaro, L. & Ranon, R. (2002b) Dynamic generation of personalized VRML content: a General Approach and its Application to 3D E-Commerce. *Proceedings of Web3D 2002: 7th International Conference on 3D Web Technology*, ACM Press, New York, pp.145–154.

Chittaro L. & Ranon R. (2000a). Adding Adaptive Features to Virtual Reality Interfaces for E-Commerce. *Proceedings of AH-2000: International Conference on Adaptive Hypermedia and Adaptive Web-based Systems*, Lecture Notes in Computer Science 1892, Springer-Verlag, Berlin, pp. 86-97.

Chittaro, L. & Ranon, R. (2000b). Virtual Reality stores for 1-to-1 E-commerce. *Proceedings of CHI 2000 Workshop on Designing Interactive Systems for 1-to-1 E-Commerce*, The Hague, The Netherlands.

Costa, R. M. E. M.; Souza, D. S. & Mendonça, I. (2010). Exploring Intelligent agents for controlling user navigation in 3D games for cognitive stimulation. *Proceedings of 8th*

International Conference on Disability, Virtual Reality and Associated Technologies - ICDVRAT, Chile, ISBN 978 07049 15022.

Dynamic-link library - DLL. Last access in September 2007. Available: http://msdn2.microsoft.com/en-us/library/ms682589.aspx

Ferber, J. (1999). *Multi-Agent Systems: An Introduction to Distributed Artificial Intelligence*, Addison-Wesley: ISBN-10: 0201360489, ISBN-13: 978-0201360486, London, UK.

Frery, A. C.; Kelner, J.; Moreira, J. & Teichrieb, V. (2002). Satisfaction Through Empathy and Orientation in Three-Dimensional Worlds. *CyberPsychology & Behavior*, Mary Ann Liebert (ed.), Vol. 5, pp. 451-459.

FIPA - Foundation for Intelligent Physical Agents. Last access in April 2011. Available: http://www.fipa.org

Java Agent DEvelopment framework - JADE. Last access in October 2007. Available: http://jade.tilab.com

Jennings, N. R. (2000). On Agent-based Software Engineering, In: *Artificial Intelligence*, Publisher: Elsevier, Volume 117, Issue 2, pp. 277-296.

Java Web Start Technology- JWS. Sun Developer Network. Last access in April 2007. http://java.sun.com/products/javawebstart

Lesser, V. R. (1999). Cooperative Multiagent Systems: a Personal View of the State of the Art. *Knowledge and Data Engineering, IEEE Transactions*, 11(1), pp. 133-142.

LipeRMI - A Light Weight Internet Approach for Remote Method Invocation. Last access in September 2007. Available: http://lipermi.sourceforge.net

Matsuba, S. N. (2007). *Interview Yumetech - Xj3D*. 3d-test - 3D temps réel et interactive. Last access in April 2007. Available: http://www.3d-test.com/interviews/xj3d_1.htm

Papatheodorou, C. (2001). Machine Learning in User Modelling. *Machine Learning and Its Applications*. Lecture Notes in Artificial Intelligence. Springer-Verlag, ISBN: 3-540-42490-3, London, UK.

Remote Method Invocation - RMI. Last access in September 2007. Available: http://java.sun.com/javase/technologies/core/basic/ rmi/index.jsp

Russell, S. J. & Norvig, P. (2010). *Artificial Intelligence: A Modern Approach*. Norfolk: Prentice Hall, New Jersey, Third edition.

Santos, C. T. & Osório, F. S. (2004). An intelligent and adaptive virtual environment and its application in distance learning. *Proceedings of the Working Conference on Advanced Visual Interfaces*. ACM Press, Gallipoli, Italy, pp. 362 - 365.

SAI - Scene Access Interface Tutorial. Last access in April 2007. Available: http://www.xj3d.org/tutorials/general_sai

Tavares, T. A.; Oliveira, S. A.; Canute, A.; Gonçalves, L. M. & Filho, G. S. (2005) A multi agent system for 3D media spaces assistance. Proceedings of *Third Latin American Web Congress*. LA-WEB 2005, ISBN: 0-7695-2471-0.

Tavares, T. A.; Araújo, A. & Souza Filho, G. (2001). *ICSpace - An Internet Cultural Space*. In: Active Media Technology. 6th International Computer Science AMT2001. Honk Kong, China, pp. 389-402.

Web3D Consortium. Open Standards for Real-Time 3D Communication. Last access in April 2007. Available: http://www.web3d.org

Wooldridge, M. (2009). *An introduction to multiagent systems* (2nd ed.), John Willey & Sons Ltd., ISBN 978-0-470-51946-2, United Kingdon.

X3D International Specification Standards. Last access in April 2011. Available: http://www.web3d.org/x3d

Xj3D - Java based X3D Toolkit and X3D Browser. Last access in April 2007. Available: http://www.web3d.org/x3d/xj3d

6

Software Agent Finds Its Way in the Changing Environment

Algirdas Sokas
Vilnius Gediminas Technical University, Department of Engineering Graphics
Lithuania

1. Introduction

Currently growing popularity of artificial intelligence technologies has evolved agent technology to develop intelligent agents. The scope of agents' use is very broad. Intelligent agents are software programs designed to act autonomously and adaptively to achieve goals defined by their human developers. These systems make use of a knowledge base and algorithms to carry out their responsibilities (Haynes et al., 2009). In the opinion of Russel and Norvig (2009), an agent is just something that perceives and acts. Dependent on their roles, skills and environment, an agent has his own capacity. In the opinion of Nwana (1996), an agents are computational systems that inhabit some complex dynamic environment, sense and act autonomously in this environment and by doing so, realize a set of goals or tasks for which they are designed.

Concept of agents leads to the early years of investigation of distributed artificial intelligence - the 1970s, particularly with Carl Hewitt "Actor" model. Hewitt suggested this model was independent, interactive and parallel treating object, which he called the "actor". The object was able to acquire some of the internal states and could respond to messages of similar objects. Actor - a computational agent, which has an e-mail address and a behavior. Characters communicate by sending messages and support their actions acting jointly, (Hewitt, 1977).

Nwana, in order to carry out a review, split all field studies of agents out into two directions: one research stream from 1977 until the date of his research (1996), the other from 1990 until the same date of the research (1996). The first one examined the direction of smart agents. This era began in the late seventies and concentrated mainly on deliberative-type agents with simple internal action models. Subsequently, Nwana identified these agents as cooperating agents. Advisory type agent is the one which has a clearly expressed symbolic world model and its decisions (for example, about what actions to perform) are based on symbolic grounds (Wooldridge, 1995).

At the beginning, the first direction focused on macro issues such as interaction and communication among agents, task decomposition, coordination and cooperation, and conflict resolution through negotiation and so on. The main objective was to define, analyze, and integrate (used in) systems, which consist of several cooperating agents. These studies have produced results in the classical systems and works, such as the "actor" model (Hewitt, 1977), MCS (Doran et al., 1991), the coordination of network activities. These agents' macro characteristics, as called by Gasser (1991), highlighted the advantages of Society of agents over the Individual agents, which are associated with micro issues. These issues are well summarized in (Chaib-draa 1992, Gasser et al., 1995) works.

In addition to the macro-level questions, the first direction of research can be also divided into the theoretical, architectural and language problems. Work related to these topics occurred naturally by exploring the macro questions. It has a very good overview by Wooldridge & Jennings (1995a) work, as well as Wooldridge & Jennings (1995b) and Wooldridge et al. (1996).

Since 1990 other software agent research and development policies clearly formed and led to a significant variety of the software agents types, which are currently being investigated. Nwana (1996) extended Wooldridge & Jennings (1995a, b) works by observing what was not included in the past era scientists work and expanded the list of the types of agents researched. Nwana states that the types and classes of agents need to be explored in addition to examining the macro topics and theory, architecture and language matters.

The agent acts independently. It is not a called component; it is an active, monitoring its environment and responsive entity. The agent monitors its environment and is able to respond to changes in a manner to be able to continue to pursue the objectives of the task. The most common goals of one agent may be narrower, so then several interacting agents are needed in order to achieve the objectives of the interest to a person or place the necessary processes. Agents can cooperate in working towards a common goal, or simply interact with each other, each to its own objectives. Exclusive multi-agents system feature is a potential opportunity to provide its global objectives. Intelligent agent is a program that reacts to the sensations of certain actions (Russel & Norvig 2009). Agent "feels" the environment and decides what actions are adequate to his senses and acts on them. Agents operate independently or nearly independently as a communication link between users and other software systems. Agents use following features: the continuity of time, autonomy, sociability, rationality, and ability to respond to the environment, adaptation. According to the architecture of agents are:

- Logic based agents. Such agents decide on action to be taken shall logical deduction method. Agent tries to make the need for action, using deductive proof. The agent is trying to prove process using deductive proof. If the formula is proved, the agent performs the act.
- Reactive based agents. These agents are simply responsive to the environment, but not reading mechanism.
- Belief-desire-intention agents. Such agents are within the beliefs, desires and intentions, and their decisions according to these three things impressions. Filtering function updates the agent's intention in accordance with its beliefs, desires and intentions of the current. Finally, the action selection function selects the most appropriate action according to the agent's intentions.
- Layers based agents. These agents take decisions during the software architectural layers. Each layer fulfill of the different levels of abstraction. There may be vertical and horizontal layers architecture. Behavior of each layer can be treated as a single agent's behavior.

This article analyzes software agent in the changing environment. Find shortest way between two points in the flat space with prominent polygon fences. This is an idealized task that a robot (agent) has to solve seeking to find its way in the environment (drawing).

The article example based on previously created technology (Sokas 2005, 2010). Graphical system can analyze drawing, forming graph, calculate graph matrices, extract route and prepare programs form with information. It discerns objects-classes: agent, graph, route, which have some properties and methods. System test is executed with drawing. Design system and example of programming agent in the drawing is presented. The creation tasks of programming agent system are solved with Agent Unified Modeling Language (AUML).

2. AUML for modeling intelligent system

Automated programming system designers use object-oriented design methods. Based on this, Unified Modeling Language (UML) was created, which is standard for describing system structure and principles of working (Rumbaugh et al., 1999). The AUML is used for designing varied programs and systems with using agent technology (Odell et al., 2000). Modeling language AUML is still being advanced today (Corchado et al., 2008; Xiao, 2009; Bajo et al., 2009; Vallejo et al., 2011).

Design system may be approached as a group of objects which members use common efforts trying to realize particular functionality. We begin to research what objects are needed for every task of user case diagrams and how these objects interact among each other.

Begin to analyze programming agent working in the drawing and collaboration of systems objects. Use case diagram for designing such type of agent has following cases: analysis of environment, graph formation, search execution, shortest way extraction and showing in the drawing. Begin to analyze only case of searching for shortest way between two points shown in the drawing. Collaboration diagram describes objects behavior in one user case zone. If user case diagrams describe the system at the end-user level, then collaboration diagram presents realization elements such as a class, objects and relationship among them. Collaboration diagram describes collection of objects, which in special situations work as united ensemble. The diagram presents ensemble's static (connections that link objects) and actions (sending messages). It accents the static ensemble structure. The messages in collaboration diagrams are numbered for showing the sending order. Collaboration diagram describes particular situation and is useful to present objective range analysis results, but is limited because we can show few messages in the diagram. Designed system user case "analysis of a drawing, graph formation, search execution, shortest way extraction and showing in the drawing" is presented in collaboration diagram (Fig. 1.).

In this collaboration diagram user controls a drawing and a form. After changing any coordinate of object point, programming agent begins to self-operate. The agent automatically analyses the drawing, forms a graph with nodes that are object points, calculates all paths from start to destination node and extracts shortest route. After that the system automatically shows this route in the graph and draws the route in the drawing and presents a form with the information.

State chart diagram describes objects' dynamic behavior only in one class (Dunn-Davies, 2005; Pan, 2009). State changes may happen because of inside transformations and actions from outside objects. We have not designed classes yet but of course a class can be a agent in the drawing. Lets analyze formation of a agent dynamics (Fig. 2.).

A software agent has three states. The first state is the analysis of a drawing, where current objects' coordinates are checked against the original ones. The first event that triggers the

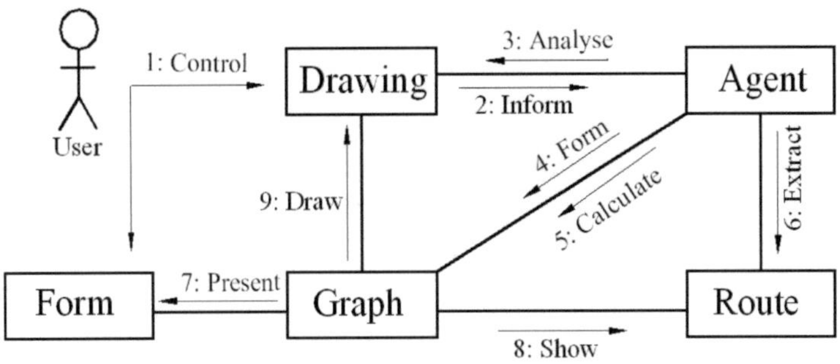

Fig. 1. System collaboration diagram

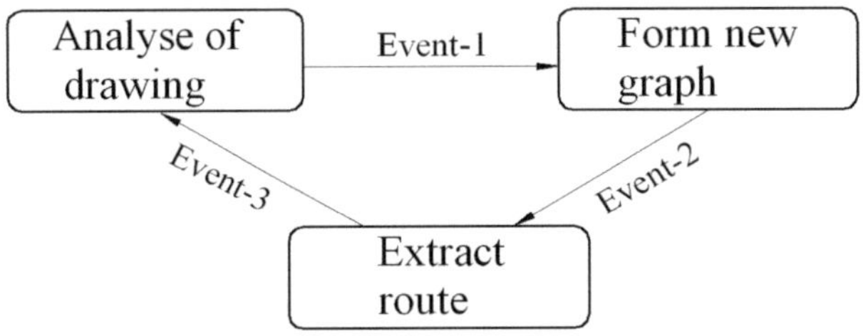

Fig. 2. Agent object statechart diagram

second state is the coordinates change of the drawing's objects. The second state is the forming of a new graph with drawing's objects. The second event that creates the third state is the new graph in the drawing. The third state is the extraction of the shortest route from the first to the end node. The third event returns to the first state but with the changed drawing and the found shortest route.

The class diagram presents static structure of a system. The agent in the drawing is composed from generalization links connected classes: agent, graph and route (Fig. 3).

All messages from collaboration diagram example for the object agent (analysis, form, calculate, extract) are presented as class operations. We will analyze class object operations in the next chapter.

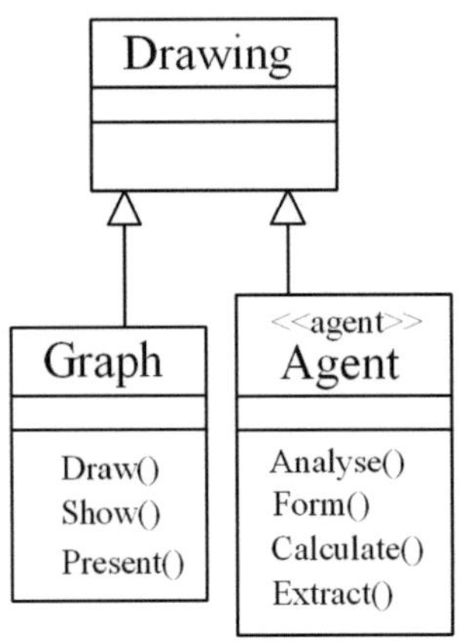

Fig. 3. System class diagram

3. Graphical objects and information

Object-oriented programming greatly facilitates a programmer's work because task is divided, as you can see from Fig 3, into two parts. Create class agent from object agent in the class diagram. All operation (analysis, form, calculate, extract) are programmed as class procedures. In this way class procedures become class methods, common variables - class properties. Graphical system AutoCAD is widely used in the world because of its open architecture and many system files that can be understood by programmers. In the system's environment, a user can operate other programming languages using standard drawing and modeling commands, creating own functions. In the AutoCAD environment we can program with Visual Basic for Applications language (VBA) (Cottingham, 2001; Sutphin, 2006).

Following operations are made by programming method: first, analyzing the drawing and identifying graphical objects. Second, all points of the drawing objects are given graph nodes assigned with numbers and the nodes are connected with edges. Third, calculating prepared matrices and getting the shortest way between all nodes of the graph. Forth, extracting the shortest path between the start and end nodes of the graph. Fifth, showing the shortest path in the graph and, sixth, drawing the shortest path. Objects in the drawing are formed of lines and present prominent polygons. Among objects are intervals. This way we can write all lines of drawing start and end point coordinates into objects matrix [*ObjM*] with method *Analyse_Drawing*:

```
For i = 0 To sk - 1
   Set obj = ThisDrawing.ModelSpace.Item(i)
   ObjM(i + 1, 1) = obj.StartPoint(0)
   ObjM(i + 1, 2) = obj.StartPoint(1)
   ObjM(i + 1, 3) = obj.StartPoint(2)
   ObjM(i + 1, 4) = obj.EndPoint(0)
   ObjM(i + 1, 5) = obj.EndPoint(1)
   ObjM(i + 1, 6) = obj.EndPoint(2)
Next
```

All information about drawing in dxf format, which is used in many graphical systems, will be studied. The data describing the entity is a list. It is made of different dxf group codes. Each such group separated by brackets also forms a list from code, dot and meaning. Code defines property, dot is a distinctive sign, and meaning is the parameter of property. For example, a list (0. "CIRCLE") informs that the code equals to zero and defines entity type, meaning is entity name. Code "-3" means that the next long list is a user extended data (Fig. 4). Additional data named extended data (xdata) may be appended to the graphical entities (Autodesk ,2001).

The next procedure are drawing graphical object the circle and creating the extended data of new graphical object. Information is named "Node". There are three extended data: number of object, circle center x coordinate and circle center y coordinate. Integer and real values are attached with codes "1070" and "1040":

```
Dim ObjCircle As AcadEntity
Dim CenterCircle(0 To 2) As Double
Dim Code1(0 To 3) As Integer
Dim Value1(0 To 3) As Variant
Set ObjCircle = ThisDrawing.ModelSpace.AddCircle(CenterCircle, 2)
```

```
Code1(0) = 1001: Value1(0) = "Node"
Code1(1) = 1070: Value1(1) = j
Code1(2) = 1040: Value1(2) = c(0)
Code1(3) = 1040: Value1(3) = c(1)
ObjCircle.SetXData Code1, Value1
ObjCircle.Update
```

Each graph node stores information about its number and coordinates. After a change in the graph, a transfer of a node to another location, information is automatically updated. Agent examines the changes and compares them with the original graph node matrix [*CM*]:

```
i=1
For Each ObjEntity In ListSelection
   ObjEntity.GetXData "Node", Code2, Duom2
   If CM(50 - i, 1) = Value2(1) Then
   If CM(50 - i, 2) <> Value2(2) Or CM(50 - i, 3) <> Value2(3) Then
      CM(50 - i, 2) = Value2(2)
      CM(50 - i, 3) = Value2(3)
   End If
   End If
   i = i + 1
Next ObjEntity
```

When the agent finds a change in coordinates of the graph nodes, it begins to operate, finding the shortest route from the initial to the end node.

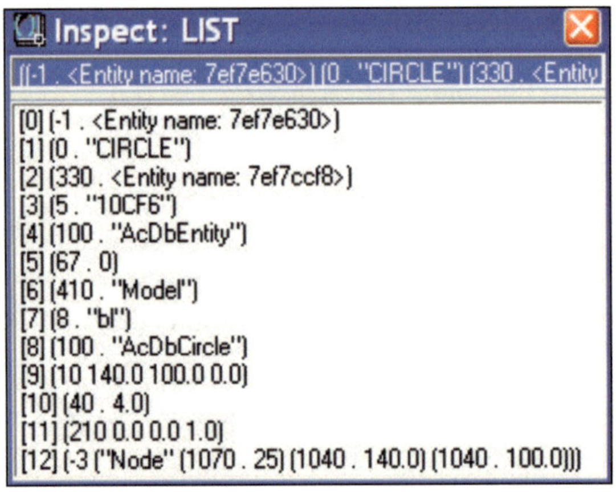

Fig. 4. Drawing interchange format for graphical object circle with extended data

4. Shortest route modeling with graph

In literature the mathematical notion graph presented as figure formed from points (or nodes, or vertex) and lines (or edges, or arcs). A graph is a pair $G = (N, E)$ of sets, where N – set of nodes, which number n is order of graph; E – set of edges, which number m is dimension of graph (Diestel, 2000). The problem is presented as non-directional graph, where edges are without directions. The path in the graph is set of nodes. The route length is equal sum of path edges lengths. Each node has some information as drawing point (coordinates). All nodes are connected by lines. These lines are shown as graph edges. Each edge also has information as drawing line (length, angle, start and end point coordinates). Literature presents several algorithms which find shortest way between two points from concrete graph node to all the other ones. They are Dijkstra, Bellman - Ford, Johnson, Floyd - Warshall algorithms. Floyd - Warshall algorithm is the simplest and fastest (Cormen et al., 2001). Floyd - Warshall algorithm is selected for finding shortest way from one graph node to another selected node. The algorithm uses intermediate node idea. It approaches path among all intermediate nodes and finds shortest route. Foundation of the algorithm is recurrent formula (1), where $d_{ij}^{(k)}$ is the shortest distance from node i to node j with intermediate node from set k =1, 2,...,n. If intermediate node is absent on the way, then the shortest distance is equal to the length of the way, or if k = 0, that $d_{ij}^{(0)} = w_{ij}$. Result of the algorithm is two symmetric and quadratic matrices n measurements: shortest way distance [*DM*] and intermediate nodes [*PM*] matrices. Matrix [*PM*] is filled in this way: if node k is on the way between i and j, then its index equals p_{ij}.

$$d_{ij}^{(k)} = \begin{cases} w_{ij}, & k = 0, \\ \min\left(d_{ij}^{(k-1)}, d_{ik}^{(k-1)} + d_{kj}^{(k-1)}\right), & k \geq 1. \end{cases} \tag{1}$$

Polygon points become nodes of the graph, and lines become edges of the graph. The method *Form_Graph* forms a graph dependent on number of nodes n, nodes matrices [*NodM*] $(n\times3)$ and it presents edges matrices [*EdgeM*] $(m\times3)$.

For calculating the graph two matrix $(n\times n)$ dimensions are presented: [*DM*] - distance between nodes and [*PM*] - intermediate nodes. The distances are determined from [*EdgeM*] with method *Prepare_Matrices:*

```
Public Sub Prepare_Matrices(n As Integer, m As Integer, EdgeM)
  For i = 1 To n
    For j = 1 To n
      If i = j Then
        DM(i, j) = 0
      Else
        DM(i, j) = 9999
      End If
      PM(i, j) = 0
    Next j
  Next i
  For i = 1 To m
    DM(EdgeM(i, 1), EdgeM(i, 2)) = EdgeM(i, 3)
    DM(EdgeM(i, 2), EdgeM(i, 1)) = EdgeM(i, 3)
  Next i
End Sub
```

Later Floyd - Warshall algorithm is used which fills matrices [*DM*] and [*PM*] with method *Calculate_Matrices*:

```
Public Sub Calculate_Matrices()
For k = 1 To n
  For i = 1 To n
```

```
        For j = 1 To n
            If (DM(i, k)+ DM(k, j) < DM(i, j)) Then
                DM(i, j)= DM(i, k) + DM (k, j)
                PMat(i, j) = k
            End If
        Next j
    Next i
  Next k
  End Sub
```

The method *Extract_Route* determines the shortest path. Method *Present Form* presents program form with calculation results and matrices.

Algorithm of shortest way between two nodes. In the cycle from graph first node until end node use method *Extract Route* which realizes following procedure:

```
Public Sub ExtractRoute (sp As Integer, ep As Integer)
  rl = DM(sp, ep)
  rs = 1
  RP(0) = sp
  RP(1) = ep
  FindPath sp, ep
End Sub
```

There *sp* – start point index, *ep* – end point index, *rl* – route length, *rs* – route size, *DM* - distance matrix, *RP* – route points vector.

Method *Find Path* finds shortest distance among start and end nodes. The algorithm of this method presented in Figure 5.

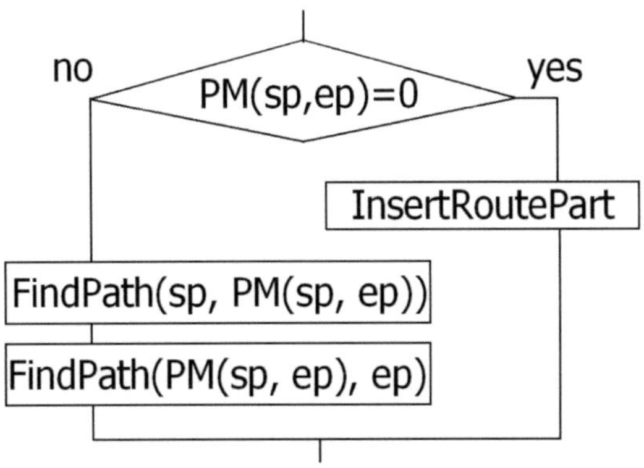

Fig. 5. Algorithm of method *Find Path*, there *PM* - path matrix, *sp* – start point index, *ep* – end point index.

The method *Find Path* which realizes following procedure:

```
Private Sub FindPath(sp As Integer, ep As Integer)
  If PM (sp, ep) = 0 Then
        InsertRoutePart sp, ep
  Else
```

FindPath sp, PM(sp, ep)
FindPath PM(sp, ep), ep
End If
End Sub

This procedure applies the recursion that is a method for the ability to call itself. This is particularly reduces the volume of program code. In recursion programs necessary to provide an output from the program, otherwise the program "hung". If the procedure calls the other procedure, it suspended its execution until the called procedure is carried out. It performs command *Exit Sub*, which applies to the next procedure.

The method *Insert Route Part* realizes following algorithm presented in Figure 6. Part of algorithm Block presented in Figure 7.

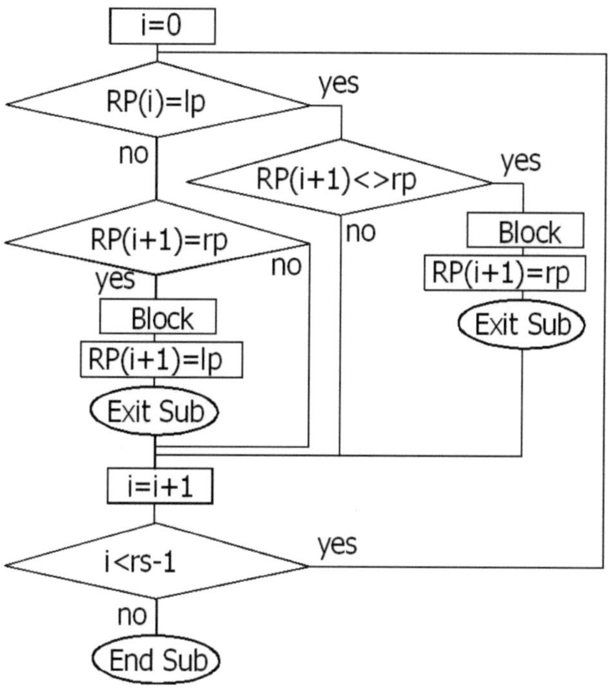

Fig. 6. The algorithm of method *Insert Route Part*

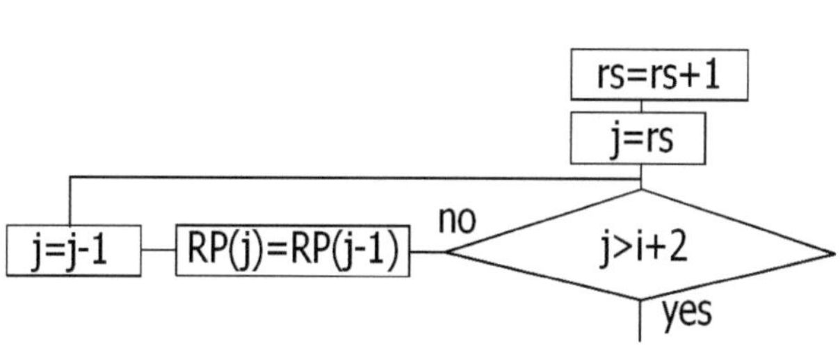

Fig. 7. Part of algorithm *Block*

The method *Insert Route Part* realizes following procedure:

```
Private Sub InsertRoutePart(lp As Integer, rp As Integer)
    For i = 0 To rs - 1
        If RP(i) = lp Then
            If RP(i + 1) <> rp Then
                rs = rs + 1
                For j = rs To i + 2 Step -1
                    RP(j) = RP(j - 1)
                Next j
                RP(i + 1) = rp
            End If
            Exit Sub
        ElseIf RP(i + 1) = rp Then
            rs = rs + 1
            For j = rs To i + 2 Step -1
                RP(j) = RP(j - 1)
            Next j
            RP(i + 1) = lp
            Exit Sub
        End If
    Next i
End Sub
```

There *lp* – left point index, *rp* – right point index, *rl* – route length, *rs* – route size, *RP* – route points vector, *i* and *j* circle indices.

5. Example

Drawing (Fig. 8) has twelve rectangles plane figures. It also indicates two extra points: 1 (start) and 50 (end). The program form (Fig. 9) shows vertices matrix, which has number column and two x and y coordinates columns. The form shows edges matrix, which first column presents edge start point numbers, second presents edge end point numbers, and the third column presents lengths of edges. The edge 2-3 is equal to 80 mm and 3-4 is equal to 30 mm, which we can see from the drawing grid, which is equal to 10 mm. From vertices and edges matrices using programming method I created 50 nodes and 105 edges graph (Fig. 10). After changing coordinates for any node, agent begins to solve the task – to find the shortest path from the first to the end node. Floyd-Warshall algorithm, for finding shortest path from one graph node to another, presents two matrices (Fig. 9). The path matrix shows from which intermediate node from node to node is the shortest way. From node 1 (first row) to node 6 (sixth column) intermediate node is 5. The length matrix presents minimum distances between concrete nodes. From node 2 (second row) to node 4 (forth column) minimum distance is 30+80=110 mm. Using path matrix the shortest path from start node 1 to end node 50 of the graph is found. The answer is in the program form (Fig. 9) top left corner: path distance and set of nodes. It is also presented in the drawings. The second drawing (Fig. 11) has changed only node 6 horizontal position by 63 mm, but result is different – another shorter path is found and distance is 439 mm. The third drawing (Fig. 12) has also changed node 6 and node 25 horizontal positions and the result is totally different – a third shorter path is found and distance is 435 mm. The fourth drawing (Fig. 13) has also changed nodes 6, 25 and 45 horizontal positions and the result is totally different – a fourth shorter path is found and distance is 424 mm.

Fig. 8. The environment drawing

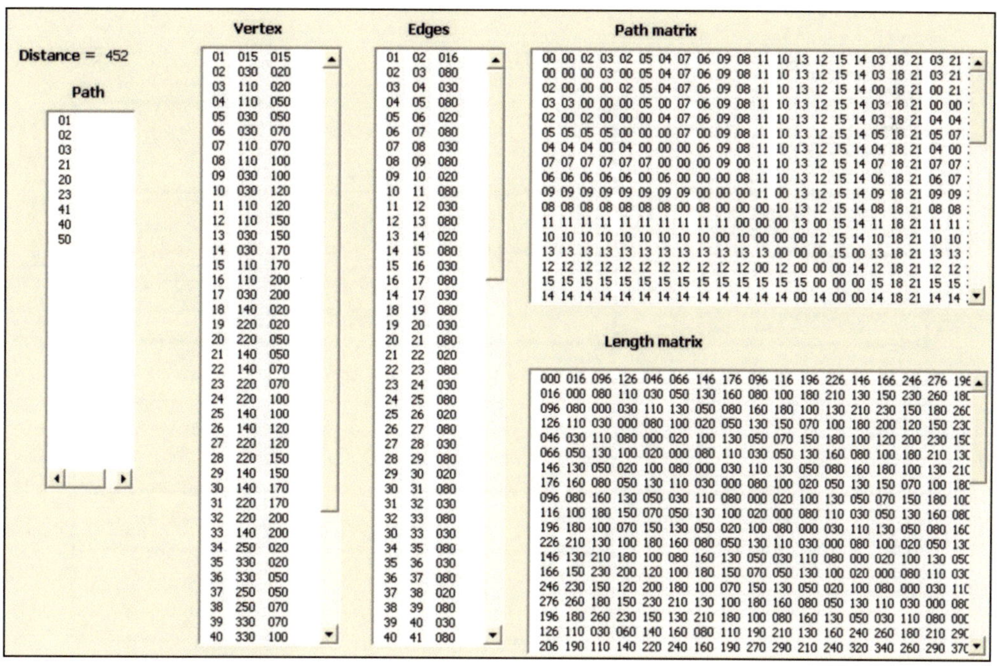

Fig. 9. The program form

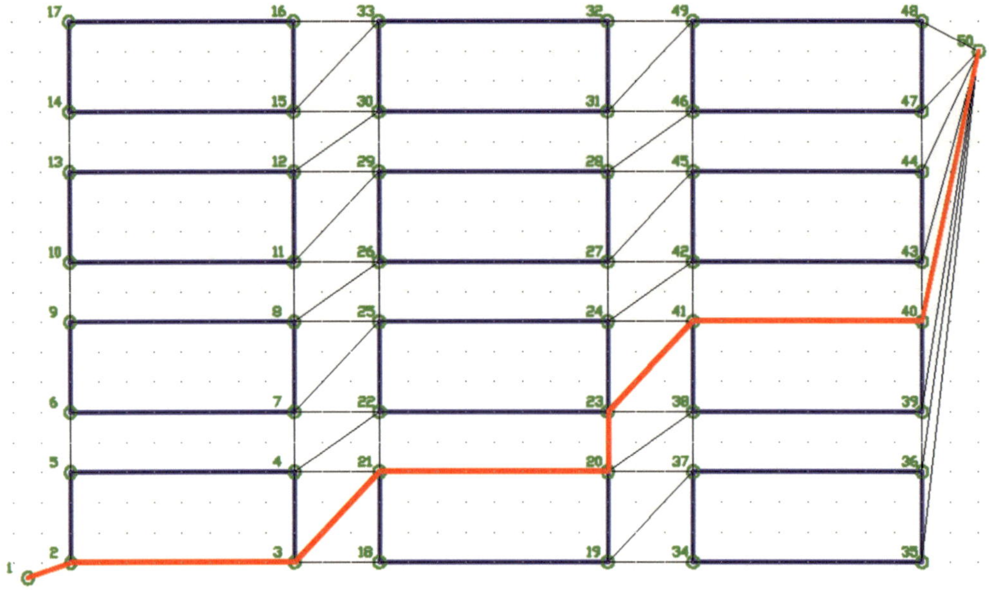

Fig. 10. First drawing

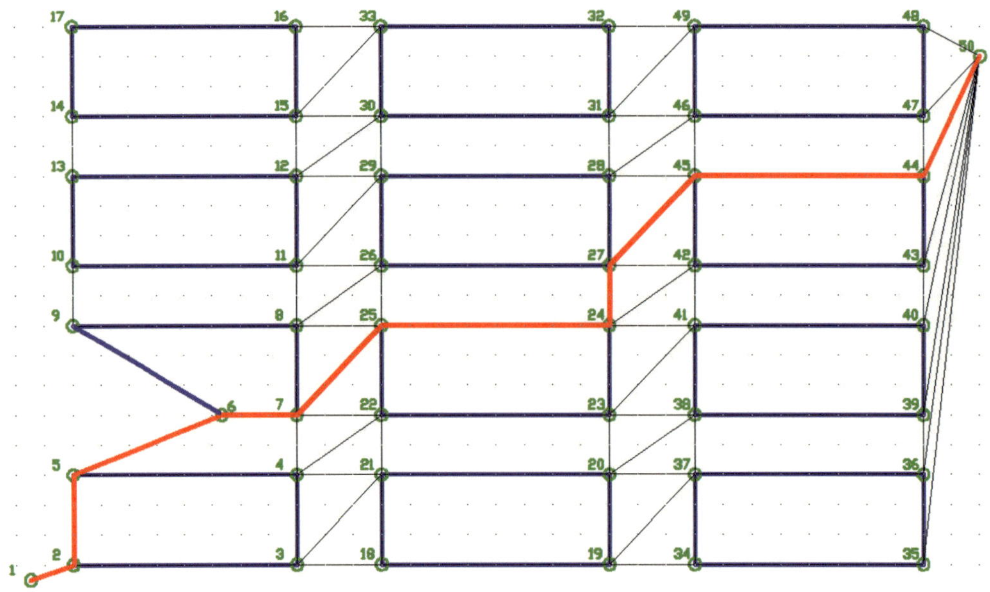

Fig. 11. Second drawing

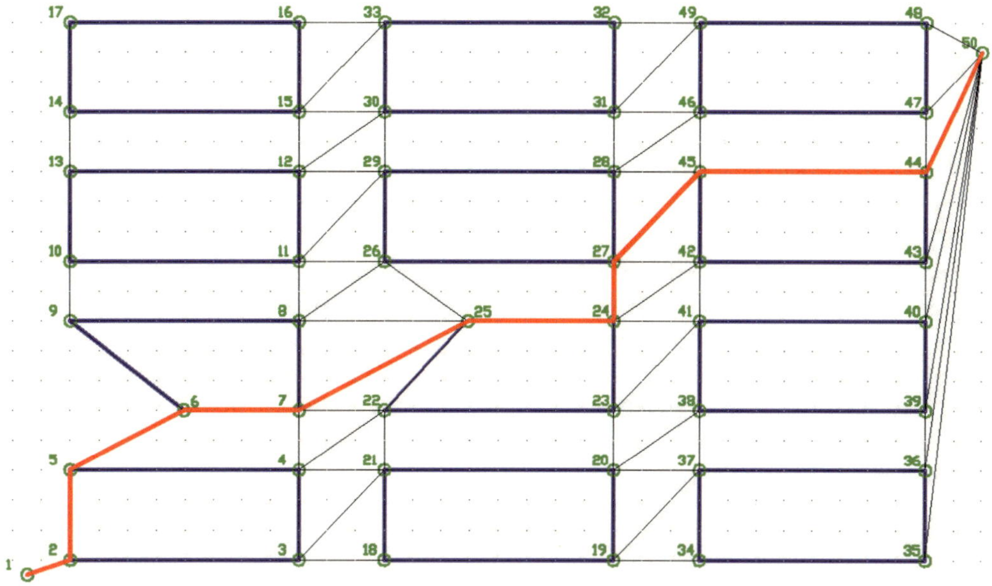

Fig. 12. Third drawing

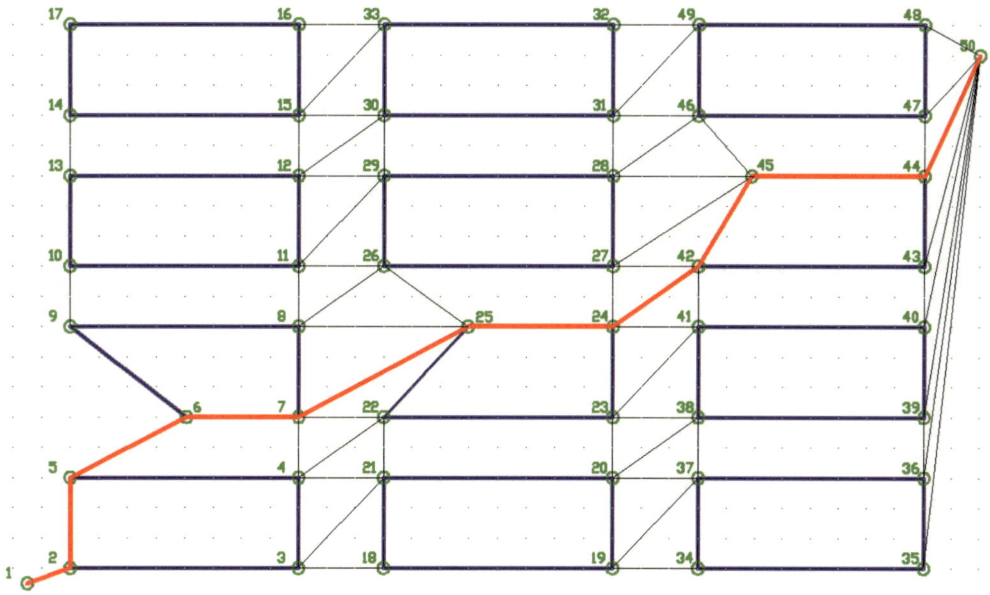

Fig. 13. Fourth drawing

6. Summary

Literature analysis indicates that software agents are used for solving different tasks and that agents are wonderful programming tool for users in the industry and science. The system is modeled by AUML. Presented project demonstrates system object classes as well as their methods and properties. It can design to individual variables activity diagrams. All of this makes programmer's work and communication with customers much easier. The object-oriented programming language, which directly allows implementation of AUML project, is used for system design. Breaking down the system into classes with specific properties and methods allows writing a program with individual modules, which simplifies and clarifies programmer's work. Two formed basic matrices help obtain an object of the graph. The vertex matrix has number column and two x and y coordinates columns. The edges matrix first column presents edges start point numbers and the second edges end point numbers, the third column presents lengths of edges. Floyd-Warshall algorithm, for finding shortest path from one graph node to another, presents two matrices. The path matrix indicates from which intermediate node from node to node is the shortest way. The length matrix presents minimum distance between concrete nodes. Using path matrix the shortest path is found from the start node to the end node of the graph. Analysis of presented graph shows that the shortest path is very sensitive to even small coordinate changes of nodes. It shows that such systems are very important for optimal control of transport and other flows. A graphical environment and a working programming language in this environment are required for design of such systems. For example, Visual Basic for Application programming language works with the AutoCAD environment.

7. References

Autodesk (2001). *AutoCAD 2002. DXF Reference Guide.* Autodesk, Inc., 188 p.

Bajo, J.; Corchado, J.M.; De Paz, Y.; De Paz, J.F.; Rodrıguez, S.; Martın, Q.; & Abraham, A. (2009). SHOMAS: Intelligent guidance and suggestions in shopping centres, *Applied Soft Computing*, Vol. 9, pp. 851–862.

Chaib-draa, B.; Moulin, B.; Mandiau, R. & Millot, P. (1992). Trends in Distributed Artificial Intelligence, *Artificial Intelligence Review* Vol. 6, pp. 35-66.

Corchado, J.M.; Bajo, J.; de Paz, Y. & Tapia, D.I. (2008). Intelligent environment for monitoring Alzheimer patients, agent technology for health care, *Decision Support Systems* Vol. 44, pp. 382–396.

Cormen, T. H.; Leiserson, C. E.; Rivest, R. L. & Stein, C. (2001). *Introduction to Algorithms,* The MIT Press, New York.

Cottingham, M. (2001). *Mastering AutoCAD VBA*, Sybex, 656 p.

Diestel, R. (2000). *Graph theory,* Electronic edition. Springer – Verlag New York.

Doran, J.; Carvajal, H.; Choo, Y; & Li, Y. (1991). The MCS Multi-agent Testbed: Developments and Experiments, *Cooperating Knowledge based Systems,* Heidelberg: Springer-Verlag, pp. 240-251.

Dunn-Davies, H. R.; Cunningham, R. J.; & Paurobally, S. (2005). Propositional Statecharts for Agent Interaction Protocols, Electronic Notes in Theoretical Computer Science, Vol. 134, pp. 55–75.

Gasser, L. (1991). Social Conceptions of Knowledge and Action: DAI Foundations and Open Systems, *Artificial Intelligence* Vol. 47, pp. 107-138.

Gasser, L. , Rosenschein, J. S. & Ephrati, E. (1995). Introduction to Multi-Agent Systems, *Tutorial A Presented at the 1st International Conference on Multi-Agent Systems*, San Francisco, CA, June.

Haynes, S. R.; Cohen, M. A.; & Ritter, F. E. (2009). Designs for Explaining Intelligent Agents, *International Journal Human-Computer Studies*, Vol. 67, pp. 90–110.

Hewitt, C. (1977). Viewing Control Structures as Patterns of Passing Messages, *Artificial Intelligence* Vol. 8, No. 3, pp. 323-364.

Nwana H. S. (1996). Software Agents: an Overview, *Knowledge Engineering Review,* Vol. 11, No. 3, pp. 205-244.

Odell, J.; Parunak, H. V.-D.; & Bauer, B. (2000). Extending UML for agents. In: *Agent-Oriented Information Systems Workshop*, 17th National Conference on Artificial Intelligence, Austin, TX, USA, pp. 3–17.

Pan, A.; Leung, S.Y.S.; Moon, K.L.; & Yeung, K.W. (2009). Optimal reorder decision-making in the agent-based apparel supply chain, Expert Systems with Applications, Vol. 36, pp. 8571–8581.

Russel, S.J. & Norvig, P. (2009). Artificial Intelligence: A Modern Approach, Prentice-Hall, third edition.

Rumbaugh, J.; Jacobson, I.; & Booch, G. (1999). *The Unified Modeling Language Reference Manual*, Addison Wesley.

Sokas, A. (2005). Data exchange technology and database in engineering drawings. *Proceedings of the Third International Conference on Construction in the 21 st Century*. Advancing Engineering, Management and Technology. September 15-17, Athens, Greece, pp. 764-769.

Sokas, A. (2010). Intelligent agent find its way in the drawing. *Solid State Phenomena: Mechatronic Systems and Materials*: a collection of papers from the 5th international conference (MSM 2009), Vilnius, Lithuania, 23-25 October 2009. Uetikon-Zurich: Trans Tech Publications Inc. Vol. 165, pp. 425-430.

Sutphin, J. (2006). *AutoCAD 2006 VBA: Programmer's Reference*. Apress, 777 p.

Vallejo, D.; Albusac, J.; Castro-Schez, J.J.; Glez-Morcillo, C. ; & Jimenez, L. (2011). A multi-agent architecture for supporting distributed normality-based intelligent surveillance, *Engineering Applications of Artificial Intelligence*, Vol. 24, pp. 325–340.

Wooldridge, M. (1995). Conceptualising and Developing Agents, In *Proceedings of the UNICOM Seminar on Agent Software,* 25-26 April, London, pp. 40-54.

Wooldridge, M. & Jennings, N. (1995a), "Intelligent Agents: Theory and Practice", *The Knowledge Engineering Review* Vol. 10, No. 2, pp. 115-152.

Wooldridge, M. & Jennings, N. (eds.) (1995b), Intelligent Agents, *Lecture Notes in Artificial Intelligence* Vol. 890, Heidelberg: Springer Verlag.

Wooldridge, M., Mueller, J. P. & Tambe, M. (1996), Intelligent Agents II, *Lecture Notes in Artificial Intelligence* Vol. 1037, Heidelberg: Springer Verlag.

Xiao, L. (2009). An adaptive security model using agent-oriented MDA. *Information and Software Technology*, Vol. 51, pp. 933–955.